SECOND EDITION

How to develop the Discipline, Attributes, and Habits that will make you a true professional

A Handbook On Becoming A TRUE Professional

CANDIDO SEGARRA

★ ★ ★ ★ ★ From the author of the acclaimed book
Are You the Architect of Your Circumstances?

Table of Contents

Acknowledgements

To my Clients:

Writing a book is a great challenge. I have been blessed with many people in my life that helped me through my professional journey, giving me a lot of experiential material to write this book. In particular, I want to thank all of my clients, past and present, which are too many to mention by name. My heart is full of gratitude and humility for the trust, friendship, and support you have given me through the years. I have learned so many valuable lessons through our association.

To my God:

He is my refuge and my fortress in whom I trust-Psalm 91

To Cathy:

My wife, best friend, and closest companion. You are a nurturer and supporter of my God given dreams. You are sensitive, loving, and genuine. I love what I am when I am with you. Thank you for being effective at the family tasks that sustain our common life. I love my experience with you.

Introduction

Pro•fes•sion: *a calling requiring specialized knowledge and often long and intensive academic preparation; b: a principal calling, vocation, or employment; c: the whole body of persons engaged in a calling.*

Pro•fes•sion•al: *engaged in one of the learned professions (1): characterized by or conforming to the technical or ethical standards of a profession (2): exhibiting a courteous, conscientious, and generally businesslike manner in the workplace.*

During my thirty-six year professional career in business, I have had the opportunity to know and work with many highly professional people, as well as with many not-so-professional individuals.

As I talk about becoming a professional, I'm not referring to specialized knowledge requiring long and intensive training in any given field. This book is about the personal attributes, qualities, characteristics, and character traits that define a person in any given position, from a janitor to a medical doctor or a rocket scientist. In other words, I'm talking about the second definition in the dictionary, not the first.

The work ethic and character trait of professionalism is fast becoming a rare commodity at every position level and in every organization. We don't learn how to become a true professional through a college curriculum, and we rarely see it modeled within many organizations today.

I was inspired to write this book for three main reasons:

1. *To help emerging generations of new professionals recognize and choose to embrace and practice the standards of professional conduct that could become their lifetime guiding principles;*

2. *To encourage experienced professionals to practice and develop skills that will lead them to new levels of professionalism by identifying the attributes that constitute true professionalism;*

3. *To resolve my personal frustration with my own shortcomings and observations of low standards and lack of professionalism in the workplace, as well as satisfy my own personal desire to become a true professional.*

I strongly believe that everyone, regardless of the career or field of choice, envisions at one point or another becoming the best that they can be in their professional career. Many people long to be admired and respected by others and identify themselves through their professions with those traits that, in their own view, make a person successful.

But few really understand what it really means to be a truly successful professional, much less how to become one. Professionalism is something that we become; it is a process determined by our habits, which shape who we are. Being a true professional is a personal character trait, not a description of our profession, how well we perform the technical aspects of our trade, how we look, or act. Professionalism is an attitude.

No matter how many years of vocational experience we may have, becoming a true professional is a personal choice and discipline as well as a personal responsibility.

In order to better understand professionalism, it is important to be able to identify what attributes and characteristics define the character traits and good habits that set a true professional apart from other people.

This book is not intended to be an encyclopedia on professional behavior, but rather a useful reference handbook, an eye opener, of the areas you should pay attention to and practice in order to become a true professional. In this new edition, I have updated or expanded some technology as well as generational and cultural points that have changed sinced the original version of the book was published.

Finally, the attributes outlined in this book are not listed in ranking order of importance. All of the attributes are important and a true professional must strive to develop them all through discipline. The apparent repetition in some chapters is intentional and is designed for learning retention in order to stress the importance of some specific points.

It is my hope that this book will influence and stimulate your thoughts as well as your resolve to become a better person and better professional.

CANDIDO SEGARRA

Watch your thoughts; they become your words.

Watch your words; they become your actions.

Watch your actions; they become your habits.

Watch your habits; they become your character.

Watch your character for it will become your destiny.

— Frank Outlaw

Attribute 1

Be on Time All the Time

The Non-Verbal Communication of Punctuality

When we practice punctuality, we are sending various unequivocal messages. First, you are communicating that you respect other people's time. Second, you are communicating that you are trustworthy. Third, you are sending a clear message that you are consistent. Fourth, it tells that you take your job seriously and that you respect yourself. Fifth, it says that you have respect for your own time and that your time is valuable too.

A true professional is always on time for appointments. Arrive to your destination at least 10 minutes early in order to relax, catch your breath, and gather your thoughts before each appointment.

Being on time for work communicates the same message of respect, trustworthiness, and consistency, which are necessary attributes if you are expecting to advance in your career and be respected in the workplace.

Plan and Schedule to Be on Time All the Time

You are expected to always be punctual, otherwise it will adversely impact your credibility. This is true whether the person you have an appointment with has the habit of arriving after the prearranged time or not.

When you schedule your appointments, block 60 minutes for a 30-minute meeting or 90 minutes for an hour meeting to allow for extended meeting time. Also leave a 30-minute time slot over the estimated driving time in-between appointments. Allowing ample time between appointments will eliminate the impolite and embarrassing position of having to cancel a scheduled appointment because your previous meetings ran over the time you allocated.

If you are running late, make sure that you call who you are meeting with to let him/her know that you are going to be late and how many minutes you are running behind. If you expect to be later than 20 minutes or more, make sure that you give the person the option of rescheduling the appointment. This shows respect and value for their time.

Show up to your meeting fully prepared and, more importantly, focused and in a mental state of readiness and alertness.

Timely Preparation Before a Meeting

A true professional finishes the tasks necessary to complete his work on time, regardless of how long it takes to accomplish it, and gives himself sufficient time to deal with unexpected problems. Never begin preparing for a meeting or start a project at the last minute. I'm certain that this bad habit did not work that well during your college years and it certainly will not serve you at all as a professional in the workplace. Always allow ample time the day before the appointment, to proofread, review, correct, and prepare for all your meetings and presentations.

It's Five O'Clock!

A professional is not looking at the clock for the quitting time, but makes sure that he completes as many tasks as possible scheduled for that day before leaving his desk. Work your day not based on the clock, but based on meeting your daily goals and tasks for the day. The key is to set realistic task-goals for each day in order to pace yourself to the early completion of each project.

A reliable person is someone who is consistently trustworthy and who is always on time and dependable to his company and coworkers. Dependability, trustworthiness, and consistency are the result of the choices that you make on a daily basis.

Etiquette means behaving yourself a little better than is absolutely essential.

— Will Cuppy

Attribute 2

Proper Business Etiquette

A true professional is always courteous, considerate, and "classy" with customers, co-workers, and other people at large. "Perception is reality," therefore, rudeness on the phone, in person, or in social events creates a perception of lack of finesse, refinement, and professionalism.

Consideration and respect for other people's time is an essential aspect of business and personal etiquette. The following are some of the key business etiquette attributes true professionals must have:

Return Your Calls!

A key aspect of business etiquette and respect is to return your telephone calls, mail, and e-mails promptly. Nothing sends a louder message of lack of care, disrespect, and rudeness than unanswered messages. If you say that you are going to return a call, return the call. Always do what you say you are going to do, when you say you are going to do it, and be consistent. You owe this to the customer, sales solicitors (yes, your potential suppliers), and to your company.

Many professionals return only those calls that may bring them the greatest benefit. Although this method can be a good time management tool, it lacks vision because the sales person calling to solicit your business could be a potential customer himself or the source of your best future customer or supplier referral. If you, out of pride or lack of sound activity management techniques, don't answer your calls even to say, "Thanks, but no thanks," you could be leaving a lot of money on the table.

In addition, not returning your communications promptly sends the unintentional message of condescendence, rudness, disrespect, pride, or even that you are disorganized and can't get around things promptly. It also sends the negative signal to the person that is trying to communicate with you that they are less important than you are and conveys a, "I'll get to you, when I can get to you," attitude.

See every caller as an opportunity, not a nuisance or an interruption because they could hide great opportunities that you could possibly be ignoring.

Perhaps a better technique is to spend the last hour of your day, or your most convenient time slot, answering all your calls and e-mails, including the sales solicitations. Ask the sales person questions about his business and his customers while you have him on the phone, and then try to sell your own products or services to him. This is what the Chamber of Commerce is all about, therefore making it a Chamber of Commerce networking moment rather than a simple sales call. You will find that this five-minute exchange could enhance your sales by at least 5%. Do you think 5% more in sales is worth your time? You bet it is!

Some years ago, an obvious sales solicitor called me and left me a voicemail. I hesitated to return the call for days. Finally, I called him back, and after a small conversation where I turned down his services, I discovered that he was connected with a large potential client. After asking him for a referral, he opened the door for me to close on an over $100,000 contract. That's how much ignoring your sales solicitors can cost you! Remember, they are trying to do their job just as much as you are trying to do yours—be a professional.

Phone Etiquette

The following are other useful tips published by the College of Business of the University of Missouri in Columbia, called Telephone Etiquette 101. You can find it at: *business.missouri.edu/341/default. aspx.*

For most of us, the telephone is a vital source of communication. The use of cell phones and "instant conversation" is commonplace in our life today. However, when applying for an internship, a permanent position, or soliciting sales, the way you conduct yourself on the phone may be a key factor in a future customer or employer's decision to do business with you.

Every time you talk on the phone, you represent the face of your company and yourself. The person on the other end of the phone cannot see you, so that person's first impression of you and your *attitude* will be determined by your tone of voice and telephone manners.

These tips will show you how paying attention to detail may make a big difference in others' impression of you, both personally and professionally.

Etiquette is the proper manner of conduct in any given setting. This includes a proper etiquette for telephone conversations. Always smile when you talk. Can you sense a smile? You bet! A positive disposition on your end of the telephone line is likely to defuse grumpiness from a caller who has a complaint.

The following are some other pointers to keep in mind when you answer the telephone:

- Identify yourself, office, or organization in as few words as possible. Try as quickly as possible to learn with whom you are speaking.

- Maintain a positive and considerate attitude toward each telephone caller. A caller easily recognizes if you seem bored or anxious to get rid of them. This is discourteous and paints a poor image of you and the organization.

- Use the telephone properly. Keep your lips about one-half to 1 inch from the mouthpiece. Pronounce letters, numbers, and names clearly. Spell out names if they could be misunderstood.

- Return calls. If you must leave the telephone during a conversation and won't be able to return immediately, say that you will call back and then follow through.

- Say "good-bye" pleasantly and replace the receiver gently.

- The person making the call should always end the conversation.

- Never take phone calls while on luncheon appointments or in the middle of a meeting, but let the voicemail take your calls.

When you talk to someone in a face-to-face setting, how much of the communicated message do you think is conveyed just by what you say and the words you use? Studies show that only 7% of a message is conveyed through the words that you use. Another 38% is carried by your tone of voice. The remaining 55% is conveyed through body language.

Obviously, this means that the most important piece of your message is not available when you're on the telephone, i.e. body language, which accounts for more than half of the communicated message that's conveyed. We must make up that missing 55% through our voice. How do you do that?

For one, be ready when the phone rings. Be prepared to talk. Give your attention to the caller — think of every call as a great opportunity waiting to happen. Set aside whatever you are doing and totally focus on what the caller is saying. Ask clarifying questions such as "What do you mean?" or "Would you like to expand on that last point?" Periodically, paraphrase their comments so you understand what the caller means, and make sure you are both on the same page. Interact with and verbally encourage the caller.

Summarizetheconversationtoclearupanyareasofmisunderstanding. Although the caller can't see them, use body gestures. Gestures allow you to be more expressive and more animated in your conversation.

Also pay attention to your vocal quality, which consists of rate, pitch, volume, clarity, and tone. Is your voice rate too fast or too slow? The average speech rate is 140 words per minute. Fast talkers come across as untrustworthy or too busy to talk. Callers may think of slow talkers as mentally slow. Pitch is the highness or lowness of your voice. High-pitched talkers tend to grate on people's nerves, while low-pitched talkers sound mechanical, almost robotic. Talk naturally, as you would normally speak in person, to avoid these problems. Volume is how loud or soft you talk. Loud people are perceived as brash and overbearing, while soft speakers are seen as shy, wimpy. Clarity takes in how your words are understood.

Dining Manners

"It May Look Like Lunch, But It's Still Business!"

The following are some additional practical tips published by the College of Business of the University of Missouri in Columbia called Rules for Business Dining:

- When inviting a client to lunch, remember that the restaurant you select is subconsciously perceived as an extension of your office. Therefore, select a restaurant where the food is of good quality and the service is reliable.

- When escorted to a table by a hostess, allow your guests to walk in front of you. When finding a table on your own, take the lead.

- Be sure to extend the power seat to your client. Seat yourself in the seat with your back facing the door/main body of the room.

- Once everyone is seated, place your napkin on your lap. This gesture serves as a cue that the meal is about to begin.

- When making a food recommendation, recognize that most guests also take your suggestion as the price range to stay within.

- When the server asks for your meal order before your guests', it's the perfect time to say, "I'd like my guests to order first." Besides being appropriate, this is a cue to let the server know that the check should be left with you at the end of the meal.

- When reaching for the bread basket, salad dressing, etc., offer them to your guests BEFORE using them yourself.

- Finally, tip adequately. Treat the server as one of your employees. It's a small price to pay for good service, personal attention, and, hopefully, the contract that you land.

I would like to add a few more useful rules:

- Like your mother told you, never talk with your mouth full.

- Never make a promise you can't fulfill.

- Speak clearly and distinctly.

- Do not gossip.

The most important thing in communication is to hear what isn't being said.

— Peter F. Drucker
American educator and writer,
b.1909, d. Nov. 2005

Attribute 3

Become a Good Communicator

Whether you communicate with one person or a full audience, the ability to convey messages and mental pictures in an organized, coherent manner to influence your audience for action is one of the most useful skills a professional can develop.

The information age has brought to the forefront the importance for professionals to be able to get their message across. Whether it is a sales or report presentation, the application of simple skills, along with lots of practice, will help you become a successful presenter. The following guidelines will help you:

1. **Define the Reason:**
    Know the reason why you are making the presentation. What is it that you want to achieve? What action do you want your audience to take? What information do you want your group to know?

2. **Do Your Research:**
    Carefully and thoroughly research the subject matter of your presentation. Get your facts right. Go online and search other people's work on the subject in order to get ideas on how to present your topic, content, etc.

Preparation of the Presentation:
The use of visual materials is an essential part of every
presentation because our minds think in pictures, visuals, and
illustrations. The following are some useful tips to prepare
your communications:

- Use PowerPoint slides, but never use more than six lines
  of copy per slide. Pay full attention to the contrast between
  your background and your fonts—a dark background with
  light color font works the best. Don't let the background
  be too distracting or busy. Use only two font types and
  two (no more than three) colors. Use animated slides and
  embedded video clips to add interest and keep the attention of
  your audience.

- Three-ring binders with clear front pocket covers are the
  most versatile way to present your handouts because you
  can customize the cover according to your presentation topic.

- If your handouts are just a few pages, try a nice presentation
  cover. Your local office supply warehouse carries many
  styles, but you can also try www.paperdirect.com for a wide
  variety of more creative, fine covers and specialized laser
  papers that are reasonably priced.

- The more white space you have in your presentation, the
  better. A handout should be a quick, easy read. When
  typing your handouts, write an outline and then go back
  and expand on each point. Use 16 or 18-point font in either
  Times New Roman or Arial to ensure easy reading.

3. Practice

Constant practice is the key to having full control of your
presentation. Your success as a presenter will depend upon the
amount of preparation and practice you allow for yourself. The
more you prepare and practice, the more confident and less
nervous you are going to be. Without such preparation, there
is sure to be failure and insecurity. The American best-selling
author H. Jackson Brown, Jr. said, "The best preparation for
tomorrow is doing your best today."

4. The Presentation

- Opening: Use a powerful attention-getter to engage your audience and get them involved from the beginning. As an opening, use natural humor or a shocking statement that is related to your presentation's theme and then explain what you meant. You can also ask a question and ask for a show of hands.

- Speaking Skills:

  1. Control your nerves before the presentation by closing your eyes and taking five slow deep breaths, slowly exhaling with each breath.

  2. Vary your voice pitch, tone, and speed.

  3. Use gestures and body movements. Be energetic, but don't exaggerate your movements—be natural.

  4. Use stories and illustrations.

  5. Use pauses to regroup or to allow your audience to digest a point you just made.

  6. Ask for opinions.

  7. Ask the audience for anecdotes, experiences, and examples related to your presentation.

  8. Make eye contact as you present in order to connect with your audience.

  9. Use the timer in your smartphone to stay on track.

  10. Involve your audience by asking questions.

- Closing:

  1. Have a powerful ending. This can be a call for action, an inspirational story, or a powerful story to help make the case of what you are presenting.

  2. Plant questions among people in the audience in order to break the ice for others to ask questions.

  3. When asked a question, repeat it in order to make sure you understand it before answering.

4. After responding to a question, make sure to ask, "Did I answer your question?" to verify the full understanding of your answer.

Influence

The art of influencing other people to action is the foundation of every presentation.

Credibility

If you don't have a "killer" resume, establish your credibility by outlining the sources of your research work. In other words, use someone else's credibility by associating and quoting them. This will let your audience know that you have done your homework in a thorough manner.

Preparation

Always over prepare. There is no substitute for solid preparation. Over preparation, solid research, and pre-meeting practice of you presentation will minimize nervousness and greatly increase confidence and control.

Demeanor

Above all, be yourself:

- Use your natural gestures and hand motions in a way that your audience perceives you as comfortable in your own skin.

- Be energetic without going overboard.

- Use humor only if you have a natural gift for humor. Otherwise, smile and be likable in a way that is very comfortable for you.

- If you make a mistake, don't highlight it by showing nervousness or using facial histrionics. Make a short pause, admit your mistake with a short statement, quickly correct it, and naturally move forward as if you meant to make the mistake.

- Vary your vocal tone, pitch, and pace of the presentation to avoid monotony.

- Make eye contact with as many members of your audience as possible.

- Always stay on schedule.

- Involve your audience as much as possible through questions, short exercises, and icebreakers.

- Include a powerful ending by telling a short inspirational story or outlining the benefits or end results of what you have presented.

- Collect feedback by encouraging questions or through evaluations.

" *The only lifelong, reliable motivations are those that come from within, and one of the strongest of those is the joy and pride that grow from knowing that you've just done something as well as you can do it.* "

— Lloyd Dobens

Attribute 4

Be Reliable

Reliability

People pay more attention to what we do, than to what we say. Be a managerial leader by example, even if you are not currently a manager or a leader. Ask yourself what healthy behaviors you admire, want to have, and would like the people around you to copy, then do those things consistently until you exemplify those behaviors.

Consistency

A consistent person is one marked by regularity of action and steady continuity in the things he says he believes or asks other people to do, free from variation or contradiction. Consistency is a choice, a habit, an attribute, and the attitude of winners.

Apply consistency by:

Always being prepared for meetings. There is nothing more unprofessional than someone who comes unprepared to a meeting or tries to "wing-it" during a presentation. There is no credible substitute for preparation.

- Always being on time to a meeting or an appointment.

- Always being honest in everything you do — not sometimes, but every time.

- Always being polite and controlled.

- Always leading and managing by example.

- Always acting on your beliefs, rather than wavering to please people.

Let a Yes be a Yes and a No be a No

You can't be truthful to other people if you are not truthful to yourself. Setting boundaries is as important and healthy in business as they are in personal relationships. Don't try to please people by telling them yes when, in reality, you mean you don't know or you feel you should say no. Setting limits is about telling the truth; it's about being truthful to others and to yourself.

In the long run, you will never burn bridges by honestly expressing your feelings behind a "yes" or a "no" answer as that shows character, honesty, integrity, and inner strength, which are attributes most people admire. Always take responsibility by meaning what you say and letting your "yes" be a "yes" and your "no" a "no."

Become a Trustworthy Person

In Luke 16:10-13 of the Bible, Jesus says that if we are honest in small things, we will be honest in big things; if we are crooked in small things, we will be a crooked in big things. He poses the rhetorical question: if we are not honest in small jobs and assignments, who will put us in charge of the store?

I think He wants us to learn that responsibility and trust are earned through responsible and trustworthy behavior. Being honest in small and large actions is a discipline to be practiced and, if done habitually, will transform us into trustworthy and reliable people as well as professionals. It's the result of our character formation, which starts with a choice of what we want to practice today.

" We Learn . . .

> *10% of what we read*
>
> *20% of what we hear*
>
> *30% of what we see*
>
> *50% of what we see and hear*
>
> *70% of what we discuss*
>
> *80% of what we experience*
>
> *95% of what we teach others. "*

— William Glasser
b.1925

Attribute 5

Learning Never Ends
for the Professional

Desire to Learn

A true professional is always striving to learn more of the technical and operational aspects of his company and constantly shows eagerness to develop his interpersonal and managerial skills.

Experts agree that in this technological world, our knowledge base doubles every three years. Our skills today will become obsolete tomorrow. The only way to stay competitive and intelligent in this rapidly changing world is by choosing to have the attitude that learning never ends for a professional.

Learning as an Attitude

Studies show that if you have the right attitude and desire to learn, the skills will follow. Learning is not an event that ends when we receive a diploma. Instead, it is a lifelong process of continuous formal and informal learning that happens by updating your skills through reading and learning from the experiences of others and your own experimentation.

Information is Power

Better yet, the wise application of information is power. When you become a well-informed person in different areas, in the professional realm as well as other, you become a source of inspiration and understanding that other people will look and be attracted to for counsel and wisdom.

Make a habit of learning about art, history, politics, theology, anthropology, science, and technology a little at a time and gradually develop an inquisitive mind for life. A good place to start is an online encyclopedia. Look for short, condensed books of different subjects in your local library. By just reading one chapter per day, you will read the whole book one bite at a time and expand your intellect.

The idea is not for you to become an expert on each subject, but for you to learn how life works.

Enroll in as many professional seminars as you possibly can and, most importantly, use them to develop an action plan, specific ideas, or programs you can implement in your workplace following each seminar.

Remember that learning is not an event, such as going to a seminar, but a process that involves a specific application plan combined with assertive action.

Intelligent conversations are based on unbiased, factual knowledge. The more educated you are on different historic, technological, cultural, political, spiritual, financial, international, cultural, and behavioral issues, the more intelligent your conversations will become. Better yet, knowledge on these issues will also heighten your critical thinking skills.

Knowledge is Competence, but Humility is Strength

It is beyond any discussion of fact that the more knowledge-competent you become, the more competent you will be in your profession. But remember that knowledge without humility becomes pride, an attribute that most people despise. The acquisition of knowledge should always be motivated and applied for the benefit of others, not to feed our own egos or to feel better about ourselves.

Learn From Other People's Experiences

Observe, listen, ask for advice, and learn from the experiences of others. This attribute not only shows strength of humility, but will save you a lot of time with your own trials and errors.

Other people's trials and errors before they achieved success is an ideal way to learn what worked and didn't work for them. Read biographies of successful people in life and in your field to profit from their experiences, their trials, perseverance, and successes and gain life context. These biographies can be not only an inspiration, but an excellent source of ideas.

Learn Through Experimentation and Risk Taking

The German classical scholar and philosopher Friedrich Nietzsche said, "The most instructive experiences are those of everyday life." Dare to experiment with ideas, explore new methods and techniques, and dare to make mistakes. Once you learn from a mistake it becomes a valuable tool in your toolbox of experience.

Team Learning

One of the characteristics of knowledge building is that the sense of "we" takes the place of the sense of "I." Team learning creates synergy—a feeling that the group operating collectively is more powerful and effective than the assembly of individuals.

A true leader leads the troops toward learning. He doesn't just send his team to a seminar, but he goes with them and they learn together. The language of humility says, "Even if I know the material, I'm going with them to coach them in order to help them understand the concepts." Many training programs don't work because the leader is not there with his team to share the concepts, supervise its application in the workplace, and coach for results, or, at the very least, lead the sponsorship of the training.

Be the kind of professional that learns with the team and applies new ideas and concepts as a unit. You will find that this is one of the smartest and most profitable ways to invest your time, even if you are a very busy individual.

You cannot climb the ladder of success dressed in the costume of failure.

— Zig Ziglar
Motivational speaker and author

Attribute 6

Dress for Credibility

You never have a second chance for a first impression. Therefore, you should always dress the part. A true professional dresses one notch above his company's code or his peers. If they are wearing golf shirts and sport pants, you should wear a sport coat, tie, and dress pants. If they are wearing sport coats, wear a nice suit.

The way you dress affects your attitude. The more informal you dress, the more informal your mindset will be.

The following are some very useful guidelines published by the College of Business of the University of Missouri in Columbia. You can find these guidelines on their website at business.missouri.edu.

Business Attire Do's & Don'ts

Looking the part promises both personal and financial success. Quality garments wear longer, fit better, and, therefore, save money in the long run. Above all, if your clothing projects a professional image, others will respond to you in kind.

Here are a few suggestions for maintaining the proper image:

MEN

- Do wear your suit jacket when you conduct business outside your office. Your authority travels with you.

- Do keep hair and nails clean and neat.

- Do wear appropriate jewelry.

- Do not overpower your appearance with heavy cologne.

- Do not wear short-sleeved shirts under suit coats—showing a clean cuff is a must.

- Do not wear ankle socks or light colored socks with a dark suit.

WOMEN

- Do wear comfortable shoes and hosiery to complement your outfit.

- Do wear natural looking makeup.

- Do wear appropriate jewelry and stay away from bangles and dangly earrings.

- Do keep hair and nails clean and neat.

- Do not overpower your appearance with heavy perfume.

- Do not wear elaborate hairstyles.

- Do not wear jeans or casual slacks.

- Do not wear trendy fashions with built-in obsolescence.

MEN

Suits: *Look for...*

- Classic fabrics, patterns, and colors that are always in style and easy to accessorize.

- Jackets with contoured collars that lie smoothly around the neck with no space between it and your shirt.

- Smooth, straight seams with a single row of stitching.

Suit care: *Be sure to...*

- Hang suits on wooden or plastic contour hangers with the jacket unbuttoned and pockets emptied.

- Leave space between hangers so garments will be free of wrinkles.

- Read and follow the care instructions on your garment.

Shirts: *The best ones have...*

- A single row of stitching along shoulder and side seams to prevent puckering.

- More stitches per inch. A quality shirt will have 15-18 stitches per inch for strength and better appearance.

- Store ties unknotted to eliminate wrinkles.

Outer coats: *Keep in mind that...*

- Outer coat sleeve length should cover the suit coat sleeve.

- You should sit in your outer coat in the store to be certain that it is comfortable.

Shoes:

- Wear shoes that coordinate with your suit.

- Keep shoes in good condition and polished.

Suits/dresses: *Look for...*

- Classic fabrics, patterns, and colors that are always in style and easy to accessorize.

- Dresses in solid colors or conservative prints.

- Jackets with contoured collars that fit smoothly around the neck with no space between it and your shirt.

- Smooth, straight seams and hems.

Suit care: *Be sure to...*

- Hang suits on wooden or plastic contour hangers with the jacket unbuttoned and pockets emptied.

- Leave space between hangers so garments will be free of wrinkles.

- Read and follow the care instructions on your garment.

Blouses/shirts: *Look for...*

- Tailored blouses/shirts with minimal frills or ruffles.

- Solid colors or conservative prints to coordinate with your suit.

Shoes:

- Wear low-heeled pumps that coordinate with your suit/dress.

- Keep shoes clean and in good condition

What is Business Casual?

- Khaki pants, neatly pressed, and a pressed long-sleeved, buttoned shirt in a solid color are a safe pairing for both men and women. Unwrinkled polo shirts are an appropriate choice if you know the environment will be quite casual, outdoors, or in a very hot location. This may not seem like terribly exciting attire. Remember, you are not trying to stand out for your cutting-edge look, but for your good judgment in a business environment.

- Shoes/Belt: Wear a leather belt and leather shoes. Please do not wear athletic shoes to a reception.

- Cost/Quality: You are not expected to be able to afford the same clothing as a CEO. However, do invest in quality clothing that will look appropriate for a business casual environment and occasions during your first couple years on the job.

- Details: Everything should be clean, well-pressed, and free from signs of wear and tear. Even the nicest khakis may not be the best choice for a reception after they've been put through the wash 100 times. Carefully inspect new clothes for tags and all clothes for loose threads, etc.

- Use common sense. If there are 10 inches of snow on the ground and you are rushing to an information session right after class, no one will expect you to show up looking ready for a photo shoot — they'll just be happy you made it. If you show up at an event and realize you are not as well dressed as you should be, make a quick, pleasant apology and then make a good impression with your interpersonal skills and intelligent questions.

- A briefcase or portfolio is not usually necessary for most business casual receptions or events.

Specifics for Men's Business Casual

- *Ties:* Ties are generally not necessary for business casual occasions, but if you are in doubt you can wear a tie. It never hurts to slightly overdress. By dressing nicely, you are paying your host a compliment. You can always wear the tie and discreetly walk by the room where the function is held. If no one else is wearing a tie, simply remove yours if you have a place to store it such as a jacket pocket.

- *Shirts:* Long-sleeved shirts are considered dressier than short-sleeved and are appropriate even in summer. Choosing white or light blue in a solid or conservative stripe is your safest bet. Polo shirts are acceptable in more casual situations, but should always be tucked in.

- *Socks:* Wear dark socks that are mid-calf length so no skin is visible when you sit down.

- *Shoes:* Leather shoes should be worn. Sandals, athletic shoes, or hiking boots are generally not appropriate for even casual events in the professional world.

- *Facial Hair:* Just as with interviews, facial hair, if worn, should be well groomed.

- *Jewelry:* Wear a conservative watch. If you choose to wear other jewelry, be conservative. Removing earrings is always a safe bet.

Specifics for Women's Business Casual

- *Pants/Skirts:* Women can wear casual pants or skirts. Neither should be tight. For the most business-like appearance, pants should be creased and tailored. If you are in doubt about the industry standard, observe women in the industry on the job, at career fairs, at information sessions, or at other related events.

- *Skirt Lengths:* Skirt length often varies from season to season. Avoid extreme trends, especially skirts with short lengths or high slits. Before choosing a skirt to wear, sit down in it facing a mirror. Be critical and ask yourself if the image is a person who looks appropriate in a business environment.

- *Shirts/Sweaters:* In addition to tailored shirts, tailored knit sweaters and sweater sets are appropriate business casual choices for women.

- *Jewelry/Accessories:* Wear a conservative watch. Jewelry and scarf styles come and go, so keep your choices simple and conservative. Avoid extremes of style and color.

- *Cosmetics:* Avoid extremes of nail length and polish color, especially in conservative industries.

- *Shoes:* Shoes should be leather or micro-fiber. Regardless of style, avoid extremes. Make certain you can walk comfortably in your shoes.

- *Hose:* Hosiery is not essential for business casual, but is recommended with shorter skirts and in more formal environments. Trouser socks or knee-high hose are appropriate with slacks.

- *Purse/Bag:* A tailored purse is best. A purse that hangs on your shoulder is advantageous, as well, because it frees your hands for greetings, such as handshakes, or holding a beverage. If you are uncertain on what to do with your purse, leaving it locked in your truck is preferable.

Ability is what you're capable of doing. Motivation determines what you do. Attitude determines how well you do it.

— Lou Holtz
Football coach
1937-1980

The longer I live, the more I realize the impact of attitude on life. Attitude, to me, is more important than facts. It is more important than the past, the education, the money, than circumstances, than failure, than successes, than what other people think or say or do. It is more important than appearance, giftedness or skill. It will make or break a company ... a church ... a home. The remarkable thing is we have a choice everyday regarding the attitude we will embrace for that day. We cannot change our past...we cannot change the fact that people will act in a certain way. We cannot change the inevitable. The only thing we can do is play on the one string we have, and that is our attitude. I am convinced that life is 10% what happens to me and 90% of how I react to it. And so it is with you ... we are in charge of our Attitudes.

— Charles R. Swindoll
American writer and clergyman

Attribute 7

Attitude

A true professional is quick with a smile, has an energetic "can-do" attitude, has a positive outlook to every situation, is eager and ready to help others, especially customers, and does what needs to be done promptly on his own initiative.

A true professional is sensitive to co-workers, is not arrogant or short-tempered, and has the ability to control and balance his ambition.

Attitude and Altitude

In life, our attitude determines how far and high in life we go, as well as where we go. Negative attitudes will bring to our reality negative results, in the same way that positive attitudes will bring to your reality positive results. Fix your attitude and you will alter your circumstances.

Learning, internalizing, and applying this principle will change your life forever. Start now.

85% of the Reason Someone is Hired and Promoted is...

Independent research studies conducted by Harvard University and the Carnegie Organization revealed that 85% of the reason why you are hired or promoted in an organization has to do with your attitude—only 15% has to do with your skills.

At our Foresight Management Development Program, we conduct an exercise where we ask managers to make a list of attributes and characteristics they look for when hiring a top manager for their organization. Invariably, 85% of what they list has to do with attitude and 15% are skills, which unequivocally proves this point.

Organizations that hire for attitude will bring aboard people with a hunger to acquire the skills necessary to succeed in the position they have been hired for.

Consideration

A person that respects and takes into consideration other people's rights, feelings, and well-being before they act is always respected and liked. Consideration toward other people shows respect, humility, and unselfishness, which are all attributes of a true professional.

Unselfishness

An unselfish attitude allows us to put other people first, over our own will-power. When we show unselfishness, we show love, respect, leadership, strength, consideration, and overall class, an attribute that is lacking in our modern society.

Courtesy

Cooperation, generosity, and good manners are the characteristics of civil behavior and professionalism. When we show respect and consideration for others, we show confidence and strength of character. We also show civility and good manners, which allows us to become the kind of person our mothers always wanted us to be.

Teaching and Delegation

A professional with the right attitude makes a point of teaching other people what he knows. He realizes that helping others grow makes him grow too. There is an old saying, "The one who teaches learns twice." As we teach and help others grow, we reinforce the skills that we have learned and become more indispensable within our organizations.

Reacting vs. Responding

This is what I call an even attitude. Most of us tend to react to other people's input, actions, communication, or circumstances, causing other people to resist us.

Reacting is emotional, while *responding* is logical. When we ask questions like, "What do you mean by that?" or, "Can you help me understand your statement?" in response to another person's reaction or criticism, you invite rationality instead of resistance because you are asking for clarification and not for a fight. This technique will also give you time to think, empathize, and truly understand what other people are feeling and meaning before you respond.

Positive Approach to Frustrations and Positive Expectations

Expect the best and have an attitude of gratitude in spite of your circumstances. It is not what happens in life, but how we chose to respond to what happens that defines our attitude. Circumstances in life are neutral—neither good nor bad.

Our mental attitudes and value-judgments based on past experiences and rooted assumptions are the reason why we label our circumstances as good or bad. We should never surrender to our circumstances, as every circumstance is a lesson in disguise and provides us with an opportunity to grow in our strenghts and weaknesses.

When we learn to see life and our circumstances with hope and optimism, we become a magnet to help and lead the way for other people who haven't learned this lesson yet.

Thoughts and Attitude Connection

Everything starts in our minds. Our most prevalent thoughts and attitudes are the builders of our habits. Our habits shape our true character, which, in turn, determines our circumstances.

The only thing we have real control over in our lives are our thoughts; we can't control people, circumstances, at least directly, or events. The only control we have is over our thought-pattern. Our thoughts trigger our emotions and our emotions control our behavior. Therefore, in order to change our behavior, we need to start with changing and focusing our mind on thoughts of goodness, joy, optimism, hope, unselfishness and, of course, love—something the world could use more of.

" The fact, in short, is that freedom, to be meaningful in an organized society, must consist of an amalgam of hierarchy of freedoms and restraints. "

— Samuel Hendel

Attribute 8

*Respect for the People
in Hierarchy of Authority*

A true professional understands structure and welcomes accountability. Therefore, a true professional is respectful and shows loyalty to the appointed chain of command, established communication channels, and protocol. By showing respect to those in authority, he shows respect for himself and sets an example for others. Remember, no company will survive without order, respect, and an authority hierarchy.

We are all accountable to someone else, whether it is to our spouses, bosses, customers, coworkers, families, friends, church pastors, parents, etc. Understanding and accepting the importance of experience and responsibility that comes with authority brings efficiency and order to any organization.

Get a Promotion by Helping Promote Your Boss

The fastest way to get a promotion is not to sabotage your boss, but to help him grow and be promoted. When we become knowledgeable, necessary contributors to the company and have a great attitude, we become candidates for promotion. If you have a boss who, in your opinion, is unfit for his job, don't sabotage his efforts. Instead, become visibly more competent than him as you help him grow, thus allowing you to show your promotion potential. Continue to do this and a promotion will become inevitable.

Order and Team Spirit

The cliché "there is no 'I' in 'team'" is a reality that few understand. When we help other people, we encourage them to help us and engage in willing participation, which will help us meet our organizational goals—that's what leadership is all about. Team spirit starts with helping others achieve their goals, so they can willingly help us achieve ours. This system never works the other way around. When we help, cooperate with, and respect other people within the organization, we promote reciprocal cooperation, willingness, and admiration from our peers and people we report to.

Dr. Robert Cialdini, a leading social scientist in the field of influence, reveals that people tend to return favors. If you help people, they'll help you. If you behave in a certain way, cooperatively, for example, they'll respond in kind. This is the same principle that operates behind Linked-In's "endorsements." Therefore, by helping others, you will be helping yourself and you will be influencing the people around you to help you achieve your goals.

The Power of a True Leader

A true professional and leader uses the power of his authority to develop and influence people, not to feed his ego with power games or to abuse people.

The power of a true leader is based on modeling positive behaviors, helping people to realize and develop their potential, and the multiplication of more leaders within the organization.

People won't resist the lines of authority if their immediate overseers are the type of people they want to become. They resist the 'jerk,' the authoritarian, the egocentric, the incompetent, the prideful, and the elitist.

Frustrations increase within organizations when we realize that some leaders want, and even demand, for us to follow them because of their titles. We don't respect hierarchies—we respect people.

A true professional and leader is a person that others gladly and confidently follow because he inspires respect (because he is respectful) and confidence (because he is trustworthy). Power is the ability to impose one's will on others, even if those others resist in some way. For a true professional and a leader, *influence* is the foundation of a healthy hierarchy, not power.

> *Knowledge comes by eyes always open and working hands; and there is no knowledge that is not power.*

— Samuel Hendel

American poet, lecturer and essayist

1803-1882

Attribute 9

Strong Knowledge of
Your Company and Its Products

A true professional engages in a constant quest for knowing more and more each day about the company's history, products, organization, and processes. The more that a professional knows about the business he is in, the more he projects professionalism and shows command of his trade.

Also, technical competence of your company's products will turn you into a more effective problem solver and a more strategic and creative thinker.

Whether it's accounting, packaging, etc., most people tend to learn as much as they can about their particular department or line of work and ignore the other functions and areas of operations. I call that attitude insular thinking. This means you are constantly focused inward and not outward.

When we go outside of our area of work to study as much as we can, I call this behavior open-minded professionalism. This includes learning the functions and processes of other departments, the functions of different people within the organization, competitive products, and the future and direction of the industry.

Don't Be Afraid to Ask Questions; Be Curious

Be a student of your company's products, your competition, and the industry you are in. Ask questions to your senior management, search the Web, download or order catalogs and brochures from competitive companies, and research trade associations for training opportunities within your industry or line of work.

Be a sponge, absorbing everything you can and learning everything that there is to learn. Learn how the products are made, different manufacturing techniques and processes, distribution channels. Learn how your competitors are marketing and advertising their products, including how their websites look. Use those reseources to find out about their pricing, merchandising, and promotions.

If you limit your scope of knowledge and training only in the area of the company you work in, you won't be able to advance quickly into other areas of the company when the opportunity knocks at your door. Many of the most successful CEOs of major companies have started from the bottom and have worked their way up by showing an attitude of eagerness to learn, even if they don't have to or haven't been asked to.

By being a student of your company and field, you will become more creative, resourceful, and useful in your workplace. Leaders pay attention to people within their organizations who show an attitude of learning, continual growth, and inquisitive minds.

Always find and make time for growing through learning, researching, training, and mentoring other people. Throughout my career, I have met many managers who never seem to have time for training, reading, or growing. Those are the people who, at the end, will spend a tremendous amount of time just keeping things as they are or innovating very little because they haven't mastered the skill of finding time to transform themselves in order to transform their organizations.

The more you know about your company, its products, its competitors, and the industry, the more essential, relevant, and trustworthy you become within your company.

" For every minute spent in organizing, an hour is earned. "

— Unknown

Attribute 10

Personal Organization Skills

A true professional knows the importance of personal and professional organization and discipline in order to be more productive, accurate in his work, and to have the ability to meet deadlines and appointments, which is a quality that is very much respected by other professionals.

A true professional recognizes the value of organization and, thus, practices the skill of working smarter and faster through it.

Clean vs. Cluttered Work Area

A cluttered work area is a reflection of a cluttered mind. A clean, uncluttered work space keeps your mind focused and will make you more productive. If we spend five minutes every hour trying to locate lost files, papers, etc., you will lose thirteen hours of productivity a month.

When our work areas are disorganized and cluttered, we tend to wander around and have disorganized thoughts.

Have a Designated Place for Everything

My father used to say, "There is a place for everything and everything has a place"—he was right. Organize your workspace, making sure that everything has a designated place. There is a vast array of storage products and office organizers to meet any need at your local office supplies store. The goal is to have everything organized in trays, storage boxes, files, etc. so you can unclutter your desk and other workspaces.

Make a habit to file or store items on a daily basis, classifying every document, letter, or file in its designated space, out of sight, as it comes to you.

Set a Specific Daily Time to Study and Grow

For a true professional, reading, whether it is a professional magazine, professional or self-help book, or report, is an important habit that keeps us relevant and updated. Choose a time when you are not tired from a long day of work to be your designated reading time. Use a well-lit area so you won't strain your eyes. Make reading an important part of your life and your habits. One of the fastest and cheapest ways of learning is by reading. The same applies to Web searches, YouTube "how to" videos, and audio books.

Browse Magazines; Cut the Articles You Want to Read and Trash the Rest

When you receive professional magazines, browse it for the articles you want to read, clip out the pages, and file them in a folder to read during your designated reading time. This practice not only helps you focus on your reading, but helps you stay organized, avoid procrastination, keeps magazines out of sight, and reduces clutter in your workspace.

Use a Label Printer

One of the tools I have found most useful is a label printer. A label printer provides a fast, easy way to print file folder labels. By using a label printer, I avoid procrastinating when opening a new file. I simply print the label, stick it to a folder, and place the document out of my sight by creating a "home" for each and every document on my desk.

Contact Management Software

One of the most effective personal and professional organization tools is the use of contact management software such as ACT or GoldMine. With good contact management software you can:

1. Schedule appointments.

2. Keep detailed notes of conversations with customers.

3. Keep all your contact information in a database that you can access in many different ways.

4. Keep TO DO lists and track your work performed and work pending.

5. Send faxes, e-mails, proposals, e-mail marketing, mail merge direct mailing, and correspondence, all attached to your contact person's electronic file.

6. Use alarms and reminders for your programmed tasks and activities.

I have used ACT for many years. It is a very intuitive and easy-to-use application, and, I assure you, it will become your best ally in customer service and customer relationships, as well as one of your most valuable time management tools.

> *Time is free, but it's priceless. You can't own it, but you can use it. You can't keep it, but you can spend it. Once you've lost it you can never get it back.*
>
> — Harvey MacKay

Attribute 11

Sharpening Your Time Management Skills

As time management experts say, the paradox of time management is that we can't manage time; we can only manage our activities. For a true professional, the wise and efficient use of time is essential to accomplish goals, enjoy life, and have an overall healthy and balanced life.

Get Organized!

The first step to manage your activities is to identify your time wasters and interruptions. Use your electronic calendar to record for one full week your current activities, day by day and hour by hour.

The second most important step is to organize yourself in a way where everything on top of your desk has a place that is very handy and easy to find. Among the ideas you may want to consider are:

1. File every important document you need for future reference. Use a small label printer to create labels fast and with ease.

2. Use a tray to file all your documents that require action and label it "TO DO."

3. Without rationalizing, trash everything else.

4. Don't allow any interruptions while you are getting organized. Completely focus on the task at hand until you finish, otherwise you will procrastinate and, most likely, you will never get it done.

5. Use a three-ring binder with dividers. Open a section on a master paper to write down all the notes hanging around your walls that are on sticky notes.

6. In another section of the three-ring binder, write a master list of all your pending projects and items that need follow-up in the form of a TO DO list.

7. Cut the articles of interest in all relevant magazines, newspapers, and periodicals in your office, open a reading file, and label it "TO READ." Trash the rest.

8. Clean your drawers, tossing everything that you haven't used in 18 months. You can also store these unneccessary items in a supply cabinet or storage room so that they are out of sight, but still organized.

9. Review your briefcase taking out all papers, letters, old documents, etc. Take the contents and file them, place them in your TO DO tray, or trash them accordingly.

10. To stay organized, clean and organize your desk before you leave at the end of the. Use the above tips to help you.

The Law of the Vital Few and the Trivial Many

In 1906, Italian economist Vilfredo Pareto created a mathematical formula to describe the unequal distribution of wealth in his country. He observed that 20% of the people in Italy owned 80% of the wealth. He soon realized that the same phenomena applied to many other disciplines as well.

The famous Pareto Principle proposes that 80% of the effects come from 20% of the causes. In other words, 20% of the essentials always accounts for 80% of the results. The key is to find out the 20% of activities that really matter and that produce 80% of the most significant results.

In Pareto's case it meant 20% of the people owned 80% of the wealth. Dr. Joseph Juran, a pioneer in quality management, stated that 20% of the defects were causing 80% of the problems. Project

Managers recognize that 20% of the work takes up 80% of your time and resources. You can apply the 80/20 Rule to almost anything, from sales to management to physics.

The value of the Pareto Principle for a manager is that it helps you realize and focus on the 20% that really matters. Of everything you do during your day, only 20% truly matters.

The key is to identify and focus on those things.

To identify your 20% vital few:

1. Make a list of the things at work that are absolutely crucial, i.e. they *must* get done.

2. Classify the list and find out how many of those activities contribute to increase sales, profit, employee development, process improvement, cost reduction, networking, innovation, or product development.

3. If something in the schedule has to be pushed and results in an unfinished task, make sure the unfinished task is not part of the 20%.

Be Discriminate With Time Spent on Web Searches

Web surfing could be one of the most powerful time wasters in your work day. Web searches that are not related to your work tasks may not only be unethical, but sometimes they consume an enormous amount of time because we get distracted surfing from one site to the next. If you must do Web searches as part of your job, leave them for the end of the day when you can do them uninterrupted. You will find your searches more focused and efficient, as you have a self-imposed time limit in order to go home.

Productive Meetings

In order to keep meetings productive, short, and to the point, the following tips may be helpful:

1. Clearly define the goal of the meeting.

2. Write and circulate an agenda in advance, requesting the documents, reports, and ideas you want them to bring to the

meeting. Define the amount of time each person will have on the agenda. Always allow sufficient time for preparation.

3. Use a recorder to keep minutes of the meeting and prepare a post-meeting follow-up list. Circulate the minutes with the follow-up and action points to all the participants.

Use of Daily Electronic Planners

Use daily electronic planner apps, which are available for any smartphone, to record all your activities for the day. These activities may be classified as:

1. **To Do**
2. **Appointments**
3. **Calls**
4. **Special Projects**

If you are using an electronic planner such as ACT, Outlook, or a phone app, make sure to use the activity alarms to alert you ahead of time when you need to make a call, leave for a meeting, or start a task. Usually, a common reason why we get to appointments late is because we don't allow ourselves enough time to quit office work and get ourselves on the road for a scheduled meeting.

Also, make sure you use the feature that automatically transfers today's undone TO DO items to the next day.

Procrastination

Procrastination is defined as intentionally putting off doing something that should be done today. Intentionally putting off something that should be done has its roots in fear. Two of the main reasons why we put off things we know we need to do today are:

- *Perfectionism: We want to make sure that all the perfect conditions are in place before we start our project. Though this is ideal, it is not a reality.*

- *Lack of Knowledge or Insecurity: When we don't know or feel insecure on how to do something, we tend to wait until we receive "divine revelation" before we start, rather than research and look for the necessary information that will teach us how to do it in a proactive way.*

As a habit, procrastination can be a major obstacle in both your career and your personal life. Procrastination is the cause of many missed opportunities and frantic, last minute work hours that cause stress and a sense of feeling overwhelmed. These feelings can escalate into resentment, guilt, and anger, which are all negative emotions you can avoid by not procrastinating.

When you think of something you have to do as a "big" project that will take up a lot of time, you will certainly put it off. Think of a project as a number of smaller pieces, or tasks, that go together like a puzzle. Address each task individually a bite at a time, rather than trying to swallow the whole chunk.

Replace the "must do" thinking with an "I'll do" attitude. "Must" implies that you are forced to do a task as if it were a duty and not a choice. Therefore, you will automatically feel a sense of heaviness, resentment, and a desire to do it when you feel more motivated. An "I'll do" attitude sends a clear message to your subconscious mind that you are in control, choosing to do the task, and that you will be successful at it. It implies that you are in control of the project, rather than the project having control over you.

A common faulty mindset that leads to procrastination is perfectionism, which is the thinking that says all circumstances have to be right in order to be able to do the job perfectly. Obviously, this perfect set of circumstances doesn't show up and we talk ourselves out of starting what we know we should do anyway.

Believing that you must do something perfectly is a cause for major stress that can easily become a vicious cycle. When this happens, you associate that stress with the task at hand and talk yourself into avoidance until the very last minute, thus causing more stress.

If we don't set a specific and realistic deadline for a task or a project, perfectionism and procrastination will cause us to delay indefinitely. Therefore, always set up realistic completion dates for each task and each project.

Another faulty mindset is the mental association that the time you spend undertaking a task or a project will take away from life's pleasures, such as watching TV, working on a hobby, or resting.. When you feel this way, combine business with pleasure. Work on a task until completion, then reward yourself with something you enjoy like going to the movies or watching your favorite TV show.

Repeat the process until the project is done. Schedule ahead of time the time you will allocate each week to family time, entertainment, exercise, social activities, personal hobbies and all your favorite leisure activities. Work your projects in small bites and reward yourself after each completion.

Another technique is to allocate a certain amount of time, two to four hours at a time, to start and finish more than one task, then reward yourself. Knowing that you have to wait only a few hours before you get the reward helps you keep going because you know you can enjoy the reward whenever you have finished the task.

By rewarding yourself for putting in the time instead of for any specific achievements, you'll be eager to return to work on your task until it is finished.

Overcoming procrastination is about reducing the mental associations of pain and increasing the mental associations of pleasure and accomplishment when beginning a task, thus gradually eliminating the inertia created by your old faulty thoughts.

Self-discipline begins with the mastery of your thoughts. If you don't control what you think, you can't control what you do. Simply, self-discipline enables you to think first and act afterward.

— Napoleon Hill
American author, 1883-1970

Discipline is the bridge between goals and accomplishment.

— Jim Rohn
American speaker and author
Famous for motivational audio
programs for business and life

Attribute 12

Discipline

Discipline is defined as the control we gain by applying orderly conduct or exercising a pattern of behavior that perfects good habits, moral character, and our mental faculties.

A true professional exercises his determination to choose self-discipline, self-control, self-regulation, self-restraint, and self-imposed order, which constitute the only path toward the achievement of any personal or professional goal. Self-discipline is control over our own weaknesses, temptations, impulses and emotions. It comes with the practice of determination, persistence, patience, restraint, and endurance.

Our habits can make us or destroy us, and the control of our thoughts is the springboard that forms our habits. By taming our thoughts, we master our habits. Only by repetition and persistence are we able to develop good habits that will shape and determine our circumstances.

Winners do what losers don't like to do, and the development of discipline is one of those things. A habit is a choice that we repeat until it becomes comfortable and part of our character.

In the same way we teach our children discipline by forcing them to do what they naturally don't want to do, we have to force ourselves to do things that we naturally don't like to do. Discipline is self-control; it is setting limits and correcting unhealthy behaviors.

When we focus our thoughts on the benefits that come from modifying our behavior, it becomes easier for us to follow through and persevere until we have mastered and conquered our habits.

With your first success in practicing self-discipline, a renewed surge of enthusiasm will propel you to the realization of your next goal in habit formation.

By exercising self-discipline, we can overcome addictions, eliminate procrastination, or overcome ignorance and poverty. Discipline is something that we develop gradually with persistence, focus, repetition, and by never giving up when we fall short.

When we were kids and wanted to learn how to ride a bicycle, we started by having a burning desire. Then we started practicing with an easier, less challenging task—riding with training wheels. This teaches you to, first, undertake easier steps where you feel confident to succeed. After we were comfortable with training wheels, we wanted to be like the "big kids" so we tried increasing the challenge by lifting the training wheels and enthusiastically practicing every day. This teaches you to not only increase the challenges in your own life, but to practice them repeatedly with perseverance.

Soon enough, we removed the training wheels and we rode the bike on our own. As we practiced more, we started practicing tricks like, "Look, mama, no hands!" This final step teaches you that confidence encourages more confidence and mastery.

The principles on developing discipline are no different than the bicycle example above. In fact, you have already successfully practiced self-discipline before, and if you apply the principle, you can conquer self-discipline and master whatever you want in life.

As you develop self-discipline, never compare yourself with others. *Pride is comparing our strength with another's weakness, and weakness is comparing ourselves with those we perceive as stronger. If you think you're weak, everyone else will seem stronger, and if you think you're strong, everyone else will seem weaker—that's human nature.*

Set your own personal goals and compare yourself only in relation to those goals and what you can accomplish. Assess and accept your present reality. If you want to lose 30 pounds, start with accepting your present weight and work a plan of disciplined dieting and exercising to realistically lose two to three pounds per week. Don't focus on the 30 pounds you want to lose, but focus on the two or three pounds you will lose this week. Soon enough, you will lose 30 pounds with minimum frustration (see Attribute 11 on procrastination).

Developing discipline is like body building or exercising— we need a plan, we need to train progressively and consistently, we need to work hard, and we must persevere, even when we fall short of the goal.

The process of self-discipline involves willpower, which is another word for determination. We must be sure of what we want and be determined to pay the price to make it become a reality.

Determination is about definitely and firmly deciding. It is the power or habit to choose to do something definitely and firmly without hesitation. Like the Nike motto says, "Just do it!"

Determination is what ignites and propels the process of self-discipline and what takes you to the starting point. It is what breaks the inertia and stops procrastination.

Discipline involves doing your work with intensity and persistence. Determination and persistence develop discipline, and sustained discipline develops endurance, or staying power. Self-discipline requires that you develop the capacity to put in the effort and the time where it's needed.

When you discipline yourself to do what seems hard and unappealing, you gain the strength denied to undisciplined people. The determination to do what seems difficult in order to meet a worthy goal is the same principle required to search for gold or diamonds; it is like having a key to a special treasure chest.

Being industrious means putting in steady, habitual effort and diligence as well as the time necessary to pursue and reach a goal. Disciplining yourself to be industrious allows you to squeeze more productivity out of your time. Time is invariable and fixed, so your personal productivity during that time is the only thing you can increase or decrease.

Persistence

Sticking to the task ahead when everyone else is ready to quit is the mark of a persistent professional. Many people abandon a task at the first signs of resistance, failure, or complications. That is why a persistent individual stands out over the crowd. Always look for different ways to accomplish and address a difficult task and don't quit until you achieve the ultimate goal. *Remember that a quitter never wins and a winner never quits!*

No human quality is more important in the accomplishment of any endeavor than persistence. My favorite definition of persistence is the ability to maintain action regardless of your feelings. This means you press on even when you feel like quitting. Persistence allows you to keep taking action when you don't feel motivated to do so and helps you achieve results, which supply and fuel more motivation and action.

Calvin Coolidge, the 30th President of the United States, eloquently said, *"Nothing in the world can take the place of persistence. Talent will not; nothing is more common than unsuccessful men with talent. Genius will not; unrewarded genius is almost a proverb. Education will not; the world is full of educated derelicts. Persistence and determination alone are omnipotent. The slogan "Press On" has solved and always will solve the problems of the human race."* Amen!

Persistence doesn't mean that you keep blindly and stubbornly doing things that don't work. Albert Einstein's definition of insanity is to *"do the same thing, the same way, over and over, expecting a different result."* Therefore, we should always be applying, adjusting, changing, and reviewing our plans, strategies, tactics, and timelines. What must stay unchanged is achievement of the goal.

By constant self-discipline and self-control you can develop greatness of character.

— Grenville Kleiser
American author 1868-1953

Attribute 13

Self-Control

A true professional and leader chooses control over anger. He chooses to respond, rather than react, and he chooses to think before taking action or rushing into judgments. A true professional postpones judgment until he can gather the facts. Leaders always praise in public and reprimand in private.

Make the habit of letting letters and e-mails of a sensitive nature rest for 24 hours before you send them. You will find that a letter you write today contains many emotions that you may find offensive tomorrow. Remember that once you put the letter in the mailbox or push the "send" button on your computer, you will not be able to take back what you said. Many relationships are irreparably broken because people reacted emotionally to situations rather than dealing with them using rational, well thought-out communication.

As I mentioned before, we can't control people or events, but we can exercise control over our own emotions as long as we allow ourselves the discipline to do so.

The first step for developing self-control is to identify those areas where you feel out of control. That could be anger, eating or drinking habits, addictions, lying, people pleasing, or overworking, just to name a few.

Second, identify the emotions and trigger points that make you more vulnerable and lead you to feel out of control.

Third, examine your self-talk process leading to your lack of self-control.

Fourth, develop new self-talk, this time rationalizing your behavior and encouraging yourself in your efforts at developing self-control (i.e. "I will not get angry with him/her. I will choose to think and respond instead of react."). Give yourself time to pause before you respond.

Fifth, develop and write down a self-talk statement for each item you want to gain control over (see first step), so you can use it every time the trigger of self-control emerges.

Sixth, prioritize the issues pertaining to the lack of self-control that need more prompt attention. Start working first with the ones that need more attention, which are the ones that affect other people the most.

Seventh, practice, practice, practice until you master it.

Always remember that the old technique of counting to ten while taking a couple of deep breaths before responding is as valid now as it has ever been. Use it, it really works!

Don't get discouraged if you start practicing self-control and you fail. As you practice the discipline of self-control, you will find yourself, at times, failing. Remember, it's going to be hard at the beginning because your old set of rooted beliefs and habits will resist the new programming. As in any endeavor in life, practice creates the habit and once you have the habit, becoming self-controlled is just a step away.

In order to see yourself achieve the success you desire in life, whether it's success in your personal life or your professional life, you must have self control. Self-control is first a choice and then an action. Apply each step of the process for developing self-control, and see yourself succeed—choose to win the battle over self!

Communication is a skill that you can learn. It's like riding a bicycle or typing. If you're willing to work at it, you can rapidly improve the quality of every part of your life.

— Brian Tracy
Author, Lecturer, and
American television host

Attribute 14

Good Communication and Presentation Skills

Of all the attributes a true professional must have in his toolbox, communication tops the list. We spend 85% or more of our awake time communicating in one way or another. We need good communications skills to connect with our spouses, our children, bosses, employees, customers, friends, and everyone we interact with.

A true professional strives to know himself and to know other people better in order to have the ability to communicate and present ideas effectively.

Listening

1. Give your total concentration and attention to the speaker. Show that you care by putting off all other activities, physical or mental. Yes, this includes no texting.

2. Show the speaker that you understand what he is saying by using verbal replies, like "I understand," "Really," and "I see," as well as responding nonverbally with nods and expressions of interest. Lean toward the speaker and make constant eye contact. Speak at about the same voice level as the other person.

3. Show that you understand what has been said by occasionally rephrasing the substance of their thought or by asking a question that shows you know the thought being expressed.

Do not constantly repeat what they've said to prove you were listening, but to show you understand what he is saying. The difference in these two intents communicates remarkably different messages to the speaker.

4. Show the speaker respect. You do this by communicating with the speaker at his level of understanding and by adjusting your tone of voice, rate of speech, and choice of words to show that you feel sympathy, understanding, and compassion for what they are saying.

Critical Dialogues

Many critical conversations pop up without warning and at the least expected moments. These conversations can range from an exchange where bets are high (like in certain negotiations), where opinions are different than ours, or where emotions are strong such as when an irate customer is shouting his complaint.

Some people typically handle these conversations by (1) avoiding them and (2) by handling them poorly because they catch them off-balance. You can handle them well if you practice a few rules that will give you the leading edge. These rules are:

1. Be Empathic

    • Restate or paraphrase what you heard the customer say.

    • Ask questions. Make the customer feel valued.

    • Increase safety by respectfully and genuinely acknowledging and mirroring the emotions people appear to be feeling.

2. Be Responsive and Proactive

    • Agree with those you are speaking to. Once you come to an agreement, move on. Don't turn an agreement into an argument.

    • Build the conversation. Say things such as, "Absolutely…In addition, I noticed that…" and then add elements that were left out of the discussion.

    • Compare differing points by saying, "I think I see things differently. Let me describe how."

3. Be Competent

    • When a customer brings a problem to our attention,
      immediately take ownership of the problem, think about a
      creative solution to the problem, and then tell them how you
      are going to resolve it.

Basic Guidelines for Designing Your Presentation

Whether you are making a sales presentation, a presentation of an
idea, a budget, a business or marketing plan, or a major speech to an
audience, there is a lot that can be quickly gained or quickly lost from a
presentation. A little bit of skill and a lot of practice will go a long way
toward making a highly effective presentation.

Organization of the Presentation

1. List the top three goals that you want to accomplish with your
    audience. Make sure that the points you want to present to
    your audience are completely clear and meet each of the goals
    you want to accomplish. It could be, and very often is, very
    easy for your audience to completely miss the point of your
    presentation for lack of focus. For example, your goals may be
    for them to appreciate the quality and features of your new
    products, learn how to use them, etc. Again, the goals are listed
    based on what you want to accomplish with your audience.

2. Clearly define who your audience is and why it is important
    for them to be at the presentation. Your audience will want
    to know right away why they were the ones invited to be at
    your presentation. Be sure that your presentation makes
    this clear to them right away. This will help you clarify
    your invitation list and design your invitation to them.

3. List the major points of information that you want to convey to
    your audience. When you're done making that list, ask yourself,
    "If everyone in the audience understands all of those points,
    will I have achieved the goal that I set for this meeting?"

4. Be clear about the mood, and emotion you want to convey
    in your presentation through your tone, for example
    hopefulness, enthusiasm, seriousness, celebration, humor,

or warning. Consciously identifying the tone you want to convey can help you project that mood to your audience.

5. Design a brief opening that takes up about 5% of your total presentation time and allows you to:

   • Present your goals and expectations for the presentation.

   • Clarify the benefits of the presentation to the audience.

   • Explain the overall layout of your presentation.

6. Develop the content and organization of your presentation. This should part should make up about 70-80% of your presentation time.

7. Prepare a brief closing of about 5-10% of your presentation time that summarizes the key points from your presentation.

8. Design time for questions and answers. This should be the remaining 10% of your presentation time.

Delivery Guidelines

1. If you're speaking to a small group of about 2-15 people, try to accomplish eye contact with each person for a few seconds throughout your delivery.

2. Prepare a presenter's outline from your presentation in font size 20, glancing at it every 5-10 seconds. Remember to look your audience most of the time, not your notes.

3. Speak a little bit louder and a little bit slower than you normally would when talking to a friend. A good way to practice these guidelines is to speak along with a news anchor when you're watching television.

4. Adjust the volume and rate of your speech and gestures to the size of your audience and age group. Lots of energy and hand gestures will work better with a younger audience, while a more sober, yet enthusiastic tone will work better with more mature audiences. Always remember that a monotone voice is absolutely poisonous for keeping the attention of an audience.

5. Stand with your feet at shoulder-length apart.

In daily communications, the expansion of the vocabulary we choose is crucial to professional success. Avoid offensive slang, street or foul language, and cursing at all cost. Street language doesn't show toughness or that you are "in," rather it shows weakness and a limited vocabulary. If you use street language, people will perceive you and treat you according to the low level of language you are using. Therefore, the first step to good communication is to improve your vocabulary, including the technical vocabulary of your industry or profession. Make a commitment to look in the dictionary and learn a new word every day.

Written Communication

The following tips can help you navigate in the world of written communication:

1. Be clear about your goal and communicate it in a short and concise manner. You must define what the goal of the communication is as well as what you are trying to achieve. For example:

    • What is the purpose of the written communication?

    • What is the specific action you want the person to take?

2. Answer the five "Ws" used in journalism to tell the story: *Who, what, where, when,* and *how.*

3. Capture the reader's attention on the first sentence of the first paragraph.

4. Use familiar words and phrases that are related to the industry you are communicating about.

5. Mention the reader's name and his company throughout the letter.

6. Avoid too many "I's" in the letter or, if possible, avoid using this word altogether.

7. Use a conversational style.

8. Explain what you want the person receiving it to do.

    • Is it to explain or clarify something?

    • Are you just sharing information or do you want a specific response from them?

9. Explain the benefits for responding as requested.

10. Always provide an encouragement or benefit for the
    reader to respond back to your communication.

11. Avoid giving the reader deadlines for the response unless it is so
    required by the circumstances or for legal purposes. Deadlines
    may sound like an ultimatum to your reader. Instead, use
    something like, "I would appreciate your prompt response."

12. Establish credibility and show respect for the reader.

13. In any written communication, be very careful about spelling,
    grammar, and punctuation. Typos are much more tolerated
    in e-mail messages than in business letters because people
    usually understand they are written quickly. However, be
    aware that many people are offended by sloppiness, so always
    re-read your message before sending it, or, better yet, let it sit
    for 24-hours and re-read it again before sending it. With this
    discipline, you may be able to separate and eliminate harmful
    emotions that you didn't see the first time around, thus saving
    yourself a lot of grief and embarrassment. Spell-checking
    your e-mail before sending it is always a wise choice.

14. Always show respectful attitudes and
    language in your communications.

15. Choose an appropriate communication method.

16. Have someone else do a quick edit and
    proofread your letter or report.

17. E-mail is quickly replacing formal business letters in many
    situations because of the quick turnaround time. Even
    so, e-mails are a more informal type of communication
    and are no substitute for formal communications.

18. The techniques described above apply when writing to
    strangers, but formal business letters are more appropriate.

19. E-mail is more adequate between people who already
    have an established relationship. However, when writing
    to someone you don't know, we suggest taking the time to
    write a formal business letter for greater effectiveness.

20. Never, never quit your job by e-mail—this is the
    coward's media of preferrence to avoid dealing with
    sensitive issues face-to-face. In this connected social
    media world, this unprofessional action may come back
    to bite you when you are searching for another job.

21. Use of Letters vs. E-mail vs. Texting

    • Use letters for formal communications or if you want to send
      a communication that will stand out from the multiple emails
      and texts your receiver gets every day.

    • Use e-mail for more informal, quick communications where
      you need instant answers or need to attach and send
      documents. E-mails are also good for confirmating and
      scheduling appointments. Never discuss crucial matters over
      email. E-mail communications don't convey emotions or facial
      expressions, therefore, your message can be misconstrued,
      misunderstood, and misinterpreted easier.

    • Use text for making quick statements or when you need
      instant, timely responses. Never have a conversation using
      texting, as professionals don't have the time to be texting back
      and forth and it becomes an interruption.

I'm a great believer that any tool that enhances communication has profound effects in terms of how people can learn from each other, and how they can achieve the kind of freedoms that they're interested in.

–Bill Gates

Attribute 15

Professional E-Mail &
Phone Communications

It is amazing to find that, in this day and age, some companies have still not realized how important their e-mail communications are. Many companies send e-mail replies late or not at all, or send replies that do not actually answer the questions asked. If your company is able to deal professionally with e-mail, you and your coworkers will obtain that all-important competitive edge that so many companies strive for. Moreover, by educating employees as to what can and cannot be said in an e-mail, you can protect your company from awkward liability issues.

Why do you need e-mail etiquette?

- A company needs to implement etiquette rules for the following three reasons:

- Professionalism: by using proper e-mail language your company will convey a professional image.

- Efficiency: e-mails that get to the point are much more effective than poorly worded e-mails.

- Protection from liability: employee awareness of e-mail risks will protect your company from costly lawsuits.

What are the E-mail Etiquette Rules?

There are many etiquette guides and many different etiquette rules. Some rules will differ according to the nature of your business and the corporate culture. Below we list what we consider as the 32 most important e-mail etiquette rules that apply to nearly all companies.

1. ***Be Concise And To The Point.***
    Do not make an e-mail longer than it needs to
    be. Remember that reading an e-mail is harder
    than reading printed communications and a long
    e-mail can be very discouraging to read.

2. ***Answer All Questions And Preempt Further Questions***
    An e-mail reply must answer all questions and preempt
    further questions. If you do not answer all the questions in
    the original e-mail, you will receive further e-mails regarding
    the unanswered questions, which will not only waste your
    time and your customer's time but also cause considerable
    frustration. Moreover, if you are able to preempt relevant
    questions, your customer will be grateful and impressed with
    your efficient and thoughtful customer service. Imagine,
    for instance, that a customer sends you an e-mail asking
    which credit cards you accept. Instead of just listing the
    credit card types, you can guess that their next question
    will be about how they can order. Go ahead and include in
    your response some order information and a URL to your
    order page. Customers will definitely appreciate this.

3. ***Use Proper Spelling, Grammar, & Punctuation.***
    This is not only important because improper spelling, grammar,
    and punctuation give a bad impression of your company,
    but it is also important for conveying the message properly.
    E-mails with no full stops or commas are difficult to read and
    can sometimes even change the meaning of the text. Besides,
    if your program has a spell checking option, why not use it?

4. ***Make It Personal.***
    Not only should the e-mail be personally addressed
    to the receiver, it should also include personal,
    customized content. For this reason, auto replies are
    usually not very effective. However, templates can
    be used effectively in this way (see next tip).

5. ***Use Templates For Frequently Used Responses.***
   Some questions you get over and over again, such as directions
   to your office or how to subscribe to your newsletter. Save
   these texts as response templates and paste these into
   your message when you need them. You can save your
   templates in a Word document or use pre-formatted e-mails.
   Even better, you can use a program such as ReplyMate for
   Outlook, which allows you to use 10 templates for free.

6. ***Answer Swiftly.***
   Customers send e-mails because they wish to receive a quick
   response. If they did not want a quick response they would
   send a letter or a fax. Therefore, each e-mail should be replied
   to within at least 24 hours, preferably within the same working
   day. If the response will take longer to write, just send an
   e-mail back saying that you have received the message and you
   will get back to them. This will put the customer's mind at rest,
   allowing them, usually, to wait patiently for your response.

7. ***Do Not Attach Unnecessary Files.***
   Sending large attachments can annoy customers and
   even bring down their e-mail system. Whenever possible,
   try to compress attachments and only send attachments
   when they are productive. Moreover, you need to have a
   good virus scanner in place—your customers will not be
   very happy if you send them documents full of viruses!

8. ***Use Proper Structure & Layout.***
   Since reading from a screen is more difficult than reading
   from paper, structure and layout are very important for e-mail
   messages. Use short paragraphs and blank lines between
   each paragraph. When making points, number them or
   mark each point as separate to keep the overview clear.

9. ***Do Not Overuse The High Priority Option.***
   We all know the story of the boy who cried wolf. If
   you overuse the high priority option, it will lose its
   function when you really need it. Moreover, even if
   an e-mail has high priority, your message will come
   across as slightly aggressive if you flag it as such.

10. ***Do Not Write in CAPITALS.***
    IF YOU WRITE IN CAPITALS IT SEEMS AS IF YOU
    ARE SHOUTING. This can be highly annoying and might

trigger an unwanted response in the form of a flame e-mail.
Therefore, try not to send any e-mail text in all capitals.

11. ***Don't Leave Out The Message Thread.***
When you reply to an e-mail, you must include the original
e-mail in your reply. In other words, click 'Reply' instead of
'New Mail.' Some people say that you must remove the previous
message since it has already been sent and is, therefore,
unnecessary. I could not agree less. If you receive many
e-mails you obviously cannot remember each individual one.
This means that a 'threadless e-mail' will not provide enough
information, and you will have to spend a frustratingly long
time finding out the context of the e-mail in order to deal
with it. Leaving the thread might take a fraction longer in
download time, but it will save the recipient much more time
and frustration in looking for the related e-mails in his inbox!

12. ***Add Disclaimers To Your E-mails.***
It is important to add disclaimers to your internal and external
e-mails in order to help protect your company from liability.
Consider the following scenario: an employee accidentally
forwards a virus to a customer by e-mail. The customer decides
to sue your company for damages. If you add a disclaimer
at the bottom of every external e-mail saying that the
recipient must check each message for viruses and that your
company cannot be held liable for any transmitted viruses,
this will surely be of help to you in court. Another example:
an employee sues the company for allowing a racist e-mail
to circulate the office. If your company has an e-mail policy
in place and adds a disclaimer to every e-mail that states
employees are expressly required not to make defamatory
statements, you have a good case for proving that the company
did everything it could to prevent offensive e-mails.

13. ***Read The E-mail Before You Send It.***
A lot of people don't bother to read an e-mail before they send
it out, as can be seen from the many spelling and grammatical
mistakes contained in e-mails. Apart from this, reading your
e-mail through the eyes of the recipient will help you send
a more effective message and avoid misunderstandings and
inappropriate comments.

14. ***Do Not Overuse 'Reply to All.'***
Only use 'Reply To All' if you really need your message to be seen by each person who received the original message.

15. ***Mailings > Use The Bcc: Field Or Do A Mail Merge.***
When sending an e-mail, some people place all the email addresses in the 'To:' field. There are two drawbacks to this practice: (1) the recipient knows that you have sent the same message to a large number of people, and (2) you are publicizing someone else's e-mail address without their permission. One way to get around this is to place all addresses in the 'Bcc:' field. However, the recipient will only see the address from the 'To:' field in their e-mail. If the 'To:' field is left blank and you do not put an e-mail address here, your message might look like spam. You could include the mailing list e-mail address in the 'To:' field, or, even better, if you have Microsoft Outlook and Word you can do a mail merge and create one message for each recipient. A mail merge also allows you to use fields in the message so that you can address each recipient personally. For more information on how to do a Word mail merge, consult the Help in Word.

16. ***Take Care With Abbreviations And Emoticons.***
In business emails, try not to use abbreviations such as BTW (by the way) and LOL (laugh out loud). The recipient might not be aware of the meanings of the abbreviations and such slang is typically not appropriate in business communications. The same goes for emoticons like the smiley :-). If you are not sure whether your recipient knows what it means, it is better not to use it.

17. ***Be Careful With Formatting.***
Remember that when you use formatting in your e-mails, the sender might not be able to view certain formats or might see different fonts than you had intended. When using colors, use a color that is easy to read on the background.

18. ***Take Care With Rich Text and HTML Messages.***
Be aware that when you send an e-mail in rich text or HTML format, the sender might only be able to receive plain text e-mails. If this is the case, the recipient will receive your message as a .txt attachment. Most

e-mail servers, however, including Microsoft Outlook,
are able to receive HTML and rich text messages.

19. ***Do Not Forward Chain Letters.***
Do not forward chain letters. We can safely say that all of them
are hoaxes. Just delete the letters as soon as you receive them.

20. ***Do Not Request Delivery And Read Receipts.***
This will almost always annoy your recipient before he
or she has even read your message. Besides, it usually
does not work since the recipient could have that function
blocked or his software might not support it. So what's
the use of using it? If you want to know whether an e-mail
was received, it is better to ask the recipient to let you
know when he receives it than to use this function.

21. ***Do Not Ask To Recall A Message.***
Biggest chances are that your message has already been
delivered and read. A recall request would look very silly
in that case wouldn't it? It is better just to send follow-up
e-mail to say that you have made a mistake. This will look
much more honest than trying to recall the message.

22. ***Do Not Copy A Message Or Attachment Without Permission.***
Do not copy a message or attachment belonging to another
user without permission of the originator. If you do not ask
permission first, you might be infringing on copyright laws.

23. ***Do Not Use E-mail To Discuss Confidential Information.***
Sending an e-mail is like sending a postcard—f you
don't want your message to be displayed on a bulletin
board, don't send it. Moreover, never make any
libelous, sexist, or racially discriminating comments
in e-mails, even if they are meant to be a joke.

24. ***Use A Meaningful Subject.***
Try to use a subject that is meaningful to the recipient as
well as yourself. For instance, when you send an e-mail
to a company requesting information about a product,
it is better to mention the actual name of the product,
e.g. 'Product A Information,' than to just say 'Product
Information' or the company's name in the subject.

25. *Use Active Voice Instead Of Passive.*
    Try to use the active voice of a verb wherever possible.
    For instance, 'We will process your order today,' sounds
    better than 'Your order will be processed today.' The first
    sounds more personal, whereas the latter, especially
    when used frequently, sounds unnecessarily formal.

26. *Avoid Using URGENT and IMPORTANT.*
    Even more so than the high-priority option, you must
    try at all times to avoid these types of words in an e-mail
    message or subject line. Only use these words if your
    e-mail is a really, really urgent or important message.

27. *Avoid Long Sentences.*
    Try to keep your sentences to a maximum of 15-20
    words. E-mail is meant to be a quick medium and
    requires a different kind of writing than formal letters.
    Also take care not to send e-mails that are too long. If a
    person receives an e-mail that looks like a dissertation,
    chances are they will not even attempt to read it.

28. *Don't Send Or Forward E-mails Containing Libelous,
    Defamatory, Offensive, Racist, Or Obscene Remarks.*
    By sending or even just forwarding one libelous or
    offensive remark in an e-mail, you and your company
    can face court cases resulting in multi-million dollar
    penalties. I assure you, in this Cyber universe we live in,
    these messages will always come back to haunt you.

29. *Don't Forward Virus Hoaxes And Chain Letters.*
    If you receive an e-mail message warning you of a new
    unstoppable virus that will immediately delete everything from
    your computer, it is probably a hoax. By forwarding hoaxes you
    use valuable bandwidth, and sometimes virus hoaxes contain
    viruses themselves, by attaching a so-called file that will stop
    the dangerous virus. The same goes for chain letters that
    promise incredible riches or ask for your help with a charitable
    cause. Even if the content seems to be legitimate, the senders
    are usually not. Since it is impossible to find out whether a
    chain letter is real or not, the best place for it is the recycle bin.

30. ***Keep Your Language Gender Neutral.***
In this day and age, avoid using sexist language such
as 'The user should add a signature by configuring his
email program.' Apart from using he/she, you can also
use the neutral gender statement 'The user should add
a signature by configuring the email program.'

31. ***Don't Reply To Spam.***
By replying to spam or by unsubscribing, you are confirming
that your e-mail address is 'live.' Confirming this will only
generate even more spam. Therefore, just hit the delete button
or use e-mail software to remove spam automatically.

32. ***Use 'Cc:' Field Sparingly.***
Try not to use the 'Cc:' field unless the recipient in the
'Cc:' field knows why they are receiving a copy of the
message. Using the 'Cc:' field can be confusing because the
recipients might not know who is supposed to act on the
message. Also, when responding to a 'Cc:' message, should
you include the other recipient in that field as well? This
will depend on the situation. In general, do not include
someone in the 'Cc:' field unless you have a particular
reason for them to see your response. Again, make sure
that this person knows why they are receiving a copy.

How do you enforce e-mail etiquette?

The first step is to create a written e-mail policy. This policy should
include all the do's and don'ts concerning the use of the company's e-mail
system and should be distributed amongst all employees. Secondly,
employees must be trained to fully understand the importance of e-mail
etiquette. Finally, implementation of the rules can be monitored by
using e-mail management software and e-mail response tools.

What are the Telephone Etiquette Rules?

The following are other useful tips published by the College of
Business at the University of Missouri in Columbia, called Telephone
Etiquette 101. You can find them at: *business.missouri.edu/341/
default.aspx.*

For most of us, the telephone is a vital source of communication.
The use of cell phones and instant conversation is commonplace in our

life today. However, when applying for an internship or permanent position, the way you conduct yourself on the phone may be a key factor in a future customer's decision to do business with you.

Every time you talk in the phone you represent the face of your company. The person on the other end of the line cannot see you, so that person's first impression of you and your attitude will be determined by the tone of your voice and telephone manners.

These tips will show you how paying attention to detail may make a big difference in others' impressions of you, both personally and professionally.

Etiquette is the proper manner of conduct in any given setting. There is also a proper etiquette for telephone conversations. Always smile when you talk. Can you sense a smile? You bet! And a positive disposition on your end of the telephone line is likely to defuse grumpiness from a caller who has a complaint.

Following are some other pointers to keep in mind when you answer the telephone:

1. **Identify Yourself, Office, or Organization in as Few Words as Possible.** Try to learn with whom you are speaking as quickly as possible.

2. **Maintain a Positive and Considerate Attitude Toward Each Telephone Caller.** A caller easily recognizes if you seem bored or anxious to get rid of them. This is discourteous and paints a poor image of you and your organization.

3. **Use the Telephone Properly.** Keep your lips about one-half to 1 inch from the mouthpiece. Pronounce letters, numbers, and names clearly. Spell out names if they could be misunderstood.

4. **Return Calls.** If you must leave the telephone during a conversation and won't be able to return immediately, say that you will call back and then follow through. As a general rule, calls should be answered either the same day or during the first part of the next day. Answering calls promptly sends the message that the person's time is respected and that the person originating the call is important. Unfortunately, the opposite is true in regards to the negative message and unprofessional image you project when you don't reply to your calls promptly.

5.   **Say "Good-Bye" Pleasantly** and
     replace the receiver back gently.

6.   **The Person Making the Call Should
     Always End the Conversation.**

7.   **Never Take Phone Calls While on Luncheon
     Appointments or in the Middle of a Meeting.**
     Instead, have the voicemail pick up your calls.

8.   **When You Talk to Someone in a Face-to-Face Setting**,
     how much of the communicated message do you think is
     conveyed just by what you say and the words that you use?
     Studies show that only 7% of a message is conveyed through
     the words you use. Another 38% is carried by your tone of
     voice. The remaining 55% is conveyed through body language.

Obviously, the most important part of your message, the body language that accounts for more than half of our communication, can't be conveyed over the phone. We must make up that missing 55% when we are on the telephone through our voice. How do you do that?

For one, be ready when the phone rings. Be prepared to talk. Give your attention to the caller and think of every call as a great opportunity waiting to happen. Set aside whatever you are doing and totally focus on what the caller is saying. Ask clarifying questions such as, "What do you mean?" or "Would you like to expand on that last point?" Periodically, paraphrase their comments so you understand what the caller means and to make sure you are both on the same page. Interact with and verbally encourage the caller.

Summarize the conversation to clear up any areas of misunderstanding. Although the caller can't see them, use body gestures. Gestures allow you to be more expressive and more animated in your conversation.

Also pay attention to your vocal quality, which consist of rate, pitch, volume, clarity, and tone. Is your voice rate too fast or too slow? The average speech rate is 140 words per minute. Fast talkers come across as untrustworthy or too busy to talk, but callers may think of slow talkers as mentally slow. Pitch is the highness or lowness of your voice. High-pitched talkers tend to grate on people's nerves, while low-pitched talkers sound mechanical and almost robotic. Talk naturally, just as you would normally speak in person. Volume is how loud or soft you talk. Loud people are perceived as brash and overbearing, while soft speakers are seen as shy, wimpy. Clarity takes in how your words are understood.

(The e-mail ettiquette section is reproduced with permission from www.emailreplies.com)

Temperance is moderation in the things that are good and total abstinence from the things that are foul.

— Frances E. Willard

Temperance is simply a disposition of the mind which binds the passions.

— St. Thomas Aquinas
Scholastic Philosopher and Theologian
1225-1274

Attribute 16

Temperance

Temperance is moderation in action. It is the restraint of indulging in appetites or passions. It is the abstinence from the use of anything that alters our state of mind, such as drugs and alcohol. It is also the control of your anger, your sexual desire outside marriage, your greed, carnal obsession, and impulses for self-gratification, such as obsessive compulsive eating.

Intemperance governs over your appetites for pleasure, while temperance is your own rational control over your unhealthy appetites. It is the conscious reprogramming of rooted assumptions and beliefs, substituting them for a new truth of good and healthy habits.

The good habit of temperance requires that you prepare and train yourself, even when you are not faced with an immediate temptation. Again, it all starts with taming your thoughts through disciplined thinking. A true professional is required to develop the habit of moderation and is expected to have control over his/her desire for pleasure and self-gratification.

A lack of moderation undermines discretion, and if discretion and trust are destroyed, all the other virtues or good habits are undermined.

Moderation itself needs to be nurtured, which is part of the responsibility of our culture. In modern society, you are constantly bombarded by images and messages of self-indulgence to appeal to your senses. The more you are exposed to these messages the more your judgment is undermined and you become convinced that self-indulgence is the portal to happiness.

The culture, with its selfish consumption messages, is directly reflected in the way you speak and act as well. A culture of lust and intemperance says, "I want it and I want it now." A culture of moderation and temperance says, "I can wait and delay the gratification for my own good," or "This is not good for me, even if it looks like fun."

A good way to practice temperance is to think of the *consequences* of your intemperate act before acting on it. Instead of indulging in the faulty thinking that an intemperate action will bring you pleasure, analyze it in a rational way and meditate on the negative consequences of the intemperate act. As you engage in this rational thinking, you will start losing the desire for intemperance as you realize that the impact and consequences of intemperance in your life are a lot harsher, more negative, and detrimental than the short term, artificial gratification you think you will experience by acting on the intemperance. It all boils down to a choice.

Intemperance comes to your life through your most prevalent thoughts, but it can also be tamed by your most prevalent thoughts. Your most prevalent thoughts will become your habits—your habits shape your character and your character determines your circumstances.

Your character, who you are when you are alone in front of a mirror, determines your current circumstances or what happens in your life. Your life and circumstances are the sum total of your choices...good or bad. It is like a checking account—your balance is equal to the deposits you make (good, unselfish, intemperate choices) minus the withdrawals you make (bad or selfish choices).

If you want to control your intemperate habits, guard your mind, because your thoughts are the roots that control and feed your actions.

Choosing the right attitude, the right thoughts, and the right actions in any circumstance requires you to develop thoughts of success and achievement as a thought-habit. Consequences are the result of choices, and those choices must include tempering your actions and your thoughts.

Bottom line, temperance versus intemperance forces you to ask yourself what choices you will make and what character you will choose to display, which, in turn, will determine the quality of your life.

There is a magnet in your heart that will attract true friends. That magnet is unselfishness, thinking of others first…when you learn to live for others, they will live for you.

— Paramahansa Yogananda

Real unselfishness consists in sharing the interests of others.

— George Santayana
Spanish-born American philosopher, poet, and humanist
1863-1952

Attribute 17

Unselfishness

Let's face it, man is essentially selfish by nature. Let me prove my point. If we have in front of us two choices, we will choose the one that is better for us, not the one that is better for humanity or the one that is better for my neighbor. It is human nature that we will choose the option that is better for ourselves.

We may have chosen an option that benefits, say, your company. But if you trace your motives you will discover that, although it benefits your company, ultimately, it will benefit you more. That was the real hidden motive of why you made the choice, not out of an unselfish virtue but for personal gain.

We may give someone a gift with the hope that it will benefit us in the future when we ask for a favor. Or we may send a note of encouragement to someone in order to maintain our reputation of being an encourager or just to feel loved. And so it goes on and on.

People have a tendency to act in ways they believe will make themselves happy or will remove discomfort from their life. Because we are all different, each individual goes about feeling good about himself or about life in general in his own particular way. In every case, the ultimate motivation is the same—to be happy. What varies between them is the definition and the means each has chosen to define and gain this happiness.

You either choose to seek happiness through selfish actions or through unselfish actions. Both the crook and the humanitarian have the same motive — to do what they believe will make them feel good. The truth is that ever since Adam and Eve's fall in the Garden of Eden, we are all selfish, it's just a matter of *degree.*

Today, selfishness is not perceived as a major issue in our society and culture because everyone selfishly seeks their own happiness as they constantly pursue their own interests.

The only way to behave unselfishly with the right motives is to perform truly unselfish acts out of gratitude for what God does for us every day, even if we don't deserve it. Just count your blessings in life and you will better understand this statement.

The reality is that our world would be much better if we would choose to work for the benefit of others. In fact, we can all find the much sought-after identity and true happiness if we just choose to be giving, unselfish, gracious, helpful, and caring. God has been all that to us and more, so we should act the same way. We teach our children to be unselfish and to share, but the truth is that many times we don't practice it ourselves.

As I say in my book *Are You the Architect of Your Circumstances?* "The world does not favor the greedy, the dishonest, the vicious, although on the mere surface it may sometimes appear to do so; it admires and helps the honest, the magnanimous, the righteous." All the great teachers of the ages have declared this in different ways.

If we pursue professionalism, we must pursue and practice unselfishness. This is a key attribute that is essential to professionals and leaders.

Do you want to enrich someone's life? Go for it — use your talents, insight, and generosity to give riches of happiness to the people God has entrusted and placed within your life. I guarantee that you'll have more genuine personal fulfillment as you discover the gift of enriching others in your life.

Unselfishness will make you a better leader, a better manager, a better father, a better husband, a better son, a better brother or sister, a better … do I need to say more?

Who is too old to learn is too old to teach.

— Proverb

*We accomplish all that we do through delegation —
either to time or to other people.*

— Stephen R. Covey

Attribute 18

Ability and Disposition to Train Through Delegation

Training and mentoring other people is an unselfish act as long as you do it with the right motive, which is to help others grow. A true professional is eager and open at all times to teach someone else what they know. The more that you teach, the more you learn; the more that you learn, the more obligation you have to teach others in return. This is the true nature of unselfish management.

A true professional must have the ability and disposition to train people through delegating relevant work. He accepts and champions other people's ideas and promotes teamwork.

Delegation is multiplication. When you delegate, you are freeing up your time to work on projects that can have more financial, product, growth, or people impact in your organization. When you delegate, you are developing other people's skills and capabilities. People will feel valued and trusted by you. New ideas and the ownership of such ideas are more likely to be generated when other people are involved in the work.

Delegation also means letting go of control and of the thinking that no one can do the job better than you. Mistakes are a great learning vehicle and a key developmental tool. Delegation is good and benefits everyone. Sometimes you may have to lower your own perfectionist standards and let people find their own solutions and ways of doing things.

Delegation is also the opportunity to give people the mentoring, teaching, and guidance they need to learn and accomplish the job, thereby developing more valuable members for your team.

The secondary, but obvious, benefit is that you will no longer be up to your neck in pending work. Delegation is a key management skill that, when practiced, will benefit the whole organization.

Delegation has five key components:

1. Review the project or task, as well as the desired end result, with the person you are delegating.

2. Give them the authority level to execute and the grace to make mistakes.

3. Negotiate and agree on the timetable and inspection points, along with when you will be making progress reviews of the project or delegated task.

4. Assure them that you are unconditionally available for help (and mean it).

5. Without being overwhelming or controlling, look over their progress (see #3).

Delegation is about directing the growth of people. It is about improving the core skills and knowledge of people in order to stay ahead of evolving trends and to improve the quality and quantity of our management teams. This effort can take place internally from people with more experience and knowledge within the organization, or externally by specialized companies with the appropriate expertise.

The internal effort, or mentoring by a trusted counselor or guide, should be a continuous responsibility and effort of the true professional. You should be in constant watch, trying to identify developmental needs you can offer to teach among peers and subordinates.

Every company should have a cross-training program. This is when you are fully trained in more than one position of responsibility. This creates flexibility and productivity improvement where everyone knows how to perform and can cover for everyone else's positions. As true professionals you should ask to be cross-trained and you should offer to be part of the teaching process.

Leadership Continuity Process

Also known as Succession Planning, Leadership Continuity Process is one of the most important functions, responsibilities, and strategic initiatives of any executive in any organization. Some large companies have specific programs to deal with talent continuity, but most small and medium- size companies don't even consider it as a priority.

The reality is that every day in the corporate world managers and executives die, resign, and retire. If you don't establish a formal process to replace their talent, you will be responsible for placing the company's future in jeopardy.

We coined the term Leadership Continuity Process over *Succession Planning* because succession has a connotation of age or something that we do shortly before someone retires, sometimes with very little formal preparation. Also, the word *planning* denotes innaction.

Leadership Continuity is an intentional action, a *process* a company will put in place to analyze your talent, assess the skills and attributes necessary to be promoted to the next level, and then train and mentor you to fill in the gaps.

Through this process you will have, at all times, fully capable managers that can fill a vacancy in short notice. Always delegate, train, and mentor the most capable person below you so you can prepare them to take your position. Do this without fear and watch your company grow along with your talent retention rates.

As a true professional, I encourage you to give serious thought to this process and chose to implement it in your organization.

The customer is our reason for being here.

— Unknown

When the customer comes first, the customer will last.

— Robert Half

If you work just for money, you'll never make it, but if you love what you're doing and you always put the customer first, success will be yours.

— Ray Kroc
*American pioneer of the
fast-food industry, founder
of McDonald's
1902-1984*

Attribute 19

Customer Experience as an Attitude

A true professional chooses to have a positive "can do-will do" attitude that separates the winners from the losers. True professionals have learned that their first loyalty is with their company, but their first duty is to the company's customers. Without satisfied, loyal customers buying from your company time and time again, your company has no future, thus, you'll have no future.

It's difficult to think of any kind of business that doesn't live or die by its customer focus. As a true professional, you have to go from just decent service to an enhanced exceptional customer experience if you want to stand out.

The **first step** of taking the challenge of becoming exceptional in your customer experience skills is the motivation to serve and help others, which goes back to Attribute 17 on unselfishness. You have to take personal ownership and constantly remember that a customer's problem is your problem.

The **second step** is to be flexible because each customer has and offers a different challenge. You have to become an expert at "plan Bs" and get comfortable with adapting to whatever comes your way by seeking creative alternative solutions.

The **third step** is to be enthusiastic and energetic at the point of contact with a customer. People love to deal with positive, enthusiastic people and are put-off by low energy, unenthusiastic people. When a customer is not happy and gets in touch with a company with enthusiastic "can-do" attitude professionals, it tends

to defuse the customer's negative attitude toward the company and they become a partner in the problem solving process.

The **fourth step** is to take ownership of your customer's situation or problem. When they call and share their problem with you, it automatically becomes your problem too. You must make clear to your customer that you are going to look for a way to solve the problem. Go above and beyond their expectations to ensure they feel as if you are part of their team—because you really are.

Finally, as Lisa Ford, one of the foremost customer service authorities in the world, says, *"Be consistent (do what you say that you are going to do, when you say you are going to do it, all the time) and be creative in serving your customer and love what you do."*

The following statistics will help show the importance and financial impact of exceptional customer service. Based on his research in the book *The Loyalty Effect*, Frederick Reichheld tells us that, depending on the industry, we can boost profits by 25-125% if we keep 5% more of our existing customers every year. He also says that if we keep just 2% more of our customers, it has the same financial impact on profits as cutting costs by 10%. Apply these numbers to your particular company situation and be surprised by how much money is at stake!

Survey studies also show that 40% of the reason why customers switch to a competitor is because of poor service or a dissapointing experience, while only 8% said it was because of cost. Therefore, customer service beyond expectation is a must if you plan to stay in business.

The lesson here is that all things must be put into consideration when running a business, even the overlooked things like an internally and externally enhanced customer experience.

Besides the profit increase that it will bring your company, exceptional customer experience determines your future successes in business and assures the loyalty of your client base.

Exceptional customer experience speaks volumes to the character of your employees, your business, and ultimately, your own character.

> *Example isn't another way to teach, it is the only way to teach.*
>
> — Albert Einstein
> *German-born physicist who developed the special and general theories of relativity*

> *A leader leads by example, whether he intends to or not.*
>
> — Anonymous

Attribute 20

Leadership by Example

Leadership is the ability of a person to influence others and to obtain their willing cooperation and personal ownership in order to achieve set goals and objectives that are required to reach a well-defined and articulated worthy vision. Leaders not only influence this journey, but they lead the way until the vision becomes a reality.

People in organizations pay more attention and follow what you *do* rather than what you *say*. There is no substitute or more powerful language than leading by example. When people start imitating the professional and human qualities and traits they see in you, the whole organization begins a path of transformation where your leadership qualities will be highly noted and appreciated.

In my definition of a leader, I stress various key qualities necessary for effective leadership:

1. A Leader Influences People

You can influence people through:

- Your character

- The authority of your position or title

- Your unique skills and talents

- Your charisma or personality

- Your age and experience

- Your historical performance

- The number of people you have served or developed

2. A Leader Persuades to Obtain Willing Cooperation

Followers are attracted and motivated by the good examples of their leaders, examples they want to emulate and follow. People are visual in nature. They interpret and follow what they see. No wonder researchers say that more than 50% of our communication comes from our body language.

Your good example is one of the most powerful training tools you possess. In fact, your character is the most powerful teaching tool you have. When people see a character trait they want in themselves, they will follow you in order to learn and obtain the desired trait they see in you.

Jesus is the best example of leading by example. In his book *The Lost Art of Leadership*, published by MileStones International Publishers, Dr. James B. Richards writes:

"The greatest leader who ever lived, Jesus of Nazareth, the Messiah, did not stand in Heaven and demand that people follow His orders. He became a man, lived among us and showed us how to live life at its fullest. His first invitation for training on His leadership team was simple: 'Follow Me!' He offered His followers the opportunity to see His teachings put into practice before deciding whether or not to accept a divine appointment. The model He lived was the proof of who He was and the process whereby He would develop His team."

For a true professional, there is nothing that will bring you more respect and recognition than to model the healthy attributes outlined in this book and to lead those around you to live them out as well.

3. A Leader Takes Personal Ownership and Responsibility

Our culture and present society is frequently characterized by people who don't want to take personal responsibility for their actions. These people spend valuable time pointing fingers, scapegoating, and giving excuses for their misconduct.

A true professional takes responsibility for his mistakes, sincerely apologizes, and take initiative to fix the mistake. Beyond this, a true professional learns from the mistake, resolves his error, and makes sure it doesn't happen again.

4. A Leader Has Clear Goals and Sets Clear Objectives

- Write down on a piece of paper everything you want to be, do, or have. Make sure the list is balanced in terms of physical, spiritual, social, career, family, and financial goals (the Five Equities of Men). This list could become pretty long.

- Let your list sit for a couple days before coming back to it. Review it and add or delete items as you see fit.

- Take each item on your list and describe it with as much detail as you can, including color, smells, size, how it feels, how it tastes, how it sounds. This technique is called "five sensing" and was originated by Walt Disney. The more rich in detail and definition, the more prone your subconscious mind will be to "buy-in" the vision.

- Set realistic timetables for the completion of each of your goals.

- Start working on the different tasks needed to accomplish the goal.

- Review this list as often as you can every week. As time goes on, rethinking your vision and adjusting your list will become necessary because some goals you originally set will lose appeal and fade into the background.

5. A Leader Has a Well-Defined and Well-Articulated Vision

Most people don't accomplish their goals because they approach them as wish lists rather than a project they have to work on. Some of us just don't believe we can accomplish big dreams and don't see the point in trying. The realization of dreams is hard work and requires a vision, a plan, strategies, timetables, daily work on the different tasks needed, periodic revision, course correction, perseverance, and, at the end, accomplishment. This may sound like a project, but that's because it is—it's your life project.

6. A Leader Guides the Way

- Encourage the team during the good and the bad.

- Cast and recast the vision, constantly keeping it in front of everyone.

- Coach the team on skills and character, serve as a sounding board, and provide the resources they need to perform at their best.

- Train the people that report to you on how to mentor and develop other people.

- Inspect what is expected.

- Personally and sincerely care for the people on your team, demonstrating that care through your actions.

7. A Leader Perseveres Until Achieving the Vision

Napoleon Hill said, *"The majority of men meet with failure because of their lack of persistence in creating new plans to take the place of those which fail."*

- Have the courage to admit when plans don't work the way you planned.

- Have the flexibility to change direction ("If at first you don't success, try another way").

- Engage your team in a brainstorming session to re-envision the plan.

- Develop detailed strategies and tactics to execute and achieve the new vision.

" Our attitude toward life determines life's attitude towards us. "

— John N. Mitchell

Attribute 21

Keep an Attitude of Excellence

A true professional has a constant commitment and attitude to do things right the first time. Such people do this because they recognize the high cost of the double effort it takes to go back to a job for a second time in order to correct mistakes and quality issues.

Excellence is the attitude or mindset of quality and of excelling. It is superiority, or the desire to be the best you can be at a high level of performance. Excellence is considered to be of great value by most organizations, but is achieved by few.

The pursuit of excellence is not to be confused with a quest for preeminence. It is also not about competition, which is based in the selfish motive of outdoing others.

Excellence is not success. Success means *being the best*. Excellence means *being your best*.

Success is about the outcome of a goal or eminence; it means being better than everyone else, like a competition.

Excellence, on the other hand, means being better tomorrow than you were yesterday. It is competing with yourself to be the best that you can be every single day.

Success means exceeding the achievements of other people. Excellence means matching what you do and who we are with the potential of what you can do or who you can be, regardless of how small or humble the task is. It is a mindset, an attitude. It is not something you do, but it is a habit.

Excellence calls for doing things right the first time. It is about practicing a skill until you master it; it's about learning new skills and upgrading the skills you already have. Excellence is about trying again and again until you have it right, making your best effort every time.

Personal excellence is about change and about taking risks. It is about making mistakes, learning from them, and correcting them; it is about loving to learn new things daily; and it is about curiosity, adaptation, and paying attention to details.

A key to excellence is to set goals and to ask for feedback, including criticism because it can help you become better every day.

Leadership by example, listening to people, and living your life with enthusiasm are all attributes of professionals who possess the attitude of gratitude and excellence.

Having fun while you are pursuing excellence is an attitude we all should practice. Encouraging others to be their best is a vital component of a team. Most of us need to be motivated and challenged to be our best, so we admire the people who take the time to care for us.

As you do your best to create a habit and an attitude for excellence, you will stumble and, sometimes, you will fall. But a man's character is measured not by the amount of times he falls, but by the amount of times he bounces back when he falls.

Your attitude of excellence can be applied to many aspects of your business, including customer service. Foresight Management Development Program coined the term Exceptional Excellence in Customer Experience©, which points to a customer experience that is not only excellent, but exceptionally excellent or beyond excellent. It is not only customer *service*, but an *experience* beyond what the customer usually may expect.

The secret of health for both mind and body is not to mourn for the past, worry about the future, or anticipate troubles, but to live in the present moment wisely and earnestly.

— Buddha

Attribute 22

Health

This chapter is not intended to be a medical treatise on health, but rather a way to create consciousness on the importance of improving your health habits in order to help your body function within the highest degree of productivity, thus, enabling you to live a fuller quality of life and high performance.

A true professional recognizes that he must stay alive and in good health in order to be productive. Self-discipline and the development of good habits in eating and exercising keeps you alert, energetic, significantly improves your attitude, and prolongs your lifespan.

Staying healthy is not a sacrifice or an optional action—it is a choice and a lifestyle. An unhealthy or a dead manager makes a poor manager in any business.

A healthy mindset starts with the attitude and awareness that you can't be happy or make anyone else around you happy without such healthy thinking.

Health is the state of balance between the absence of illness (normal body functions), the ability to cope with your environment and daily life (stress levels and psychological state), and your personal physical fitness (optimum body wellness and function). The combination of these factors determines a healthy quality of life.

Health is maintained and improved through physical fitness, weight loss, healthy eating, stress management training, and avoiding smoking and abusing other harmful substances. The science and practice of medicine can definitely improve health, especially when your state of wellness is threatened or in danger.

Dr. John Tickell, a world-renowned medical researcher in the area of stress, says, *"Stress is predictable and preventable. We all have the external pressures that life brings: mortgage payments that are due, personal conflicts, loss of love or a loved one, deadlines, etc. I call those external pressures opposing forces, as generally speaking, you don't necessarily want those events to happen, but they happen and you can't control them."*

You can choose to *respond* or *react* to such external opposing forces or pressures. If you choose to react, it means you have chosen to reply by using an emotion such as anger, sadness, indignation, love, or fear. If you choose to respond to the pressures of life, it means that you have chosen to be more rational, taking the time to look for explanations and understand the source and reasons of the pressures before you formulate any type of response.

In both cases you have little or no control over the pressures of life, but you do have control over the choice that you make on how to deal with those pressures. Either you choose to emotionally react or rationally respond—it's your choice. The choice that you make in this area determines the amount and intensity of stress you live your life under, as well as the strain you submit your body and immune system to.

Fear and worry are significant factors that destroy inner peace and bring disharmony and stress. Emotional responses can be caused by anticipation or awareness of danger. Fears can be real, such as a truck coming your way, or irrational, such as feeling a pain in your chest and thinking, "What if I'm having a heart attack or have lung cancer?" Real fears are a useful tool because they help you avoid danger, but irrational fears only serve to paralyze you from functioning properly in this world.

Worrying is thinking and dwelling on the things you *don't* want to happen, which leads to feelings of fear. When we think and dwell on the things we *do* want to happen instead of worrying about those we don't, we become less stress and feel emotions of hope, peace, and positivity.

Everybody has faith in something. If it is faith in yourself exclusively, then you will have a very limited view of what you can and cannot do. If your faith is in God who created and maintains control over the universe and the complexities of the human body, your view of what you can or can't do as His instrument could be, I believe, unlimited.

If you feel as if you have to control everything in your life, you will live in a constant state of stress, worry, and fear. But if you believe that the Creator of everything is actually in control and that He is on call to hear your needs and help you, as long as you trust Him and let Him work, He will give you a peace and confidence like none you have ever experienced before. Studies show that people who believe in something greater than themselves, i.e. God, are healthier, happier, and heal faster than the people who believe they are their own god or that there is no God.

We all act on our beliefs. We become who we are based on our most prevalent thoughts. Therefore, you must feed yourself with the right thoughts and belief system in order to fill your mind with the self-affirmations and positive thoughts you need to get you where you want to be in life.

This applies to not just what we put in our minds, but what we put in our bodies as well. In the same way that what you put in an engine determines how well it will run, what you eat determines how well your body function. Healthy, balanced meals containing proteins, carbohydrates, and fiber in moderate portions will increase your energy, keep your body healthier, and increase your lifespan. You will also be more alert, think faster and more clearly, be able work longer hours without getting tired, and have a better attitude.

Exercise is also an essential health component. Make sure you spend at least 30 minutes, 3 times a week, in some kind of physical activity. More would be better, but this is the minimum recommended amount. Running, lifting weights, or walking on a treadmill are excellent ways to increase your metabolism rate and strengthen your heart.

Major health killers include fear and worry, addictions and chemical dependencies, anger, poor eating habits, sleep deprivation, lack of exercise, overwork, and lack of inner peace, among others.

You cannot live your life without the help of the people and things around you bringing balance to your life. Simply put, taking time to maintain a healthy lifestyle through exercise, healthy eating habits, and faith in God provides an environment for you and those around you to thrive in. When you reduce worry and stress in your daily routines, you will find the joy that will bring you long-lasting life.

Teamwork is the ability to work together toward a common vision. The ability to direct individual accomplishments toward organizational objectives. It is the fuel that allows common people to attain uncommon results.

— Unknown

Attribute 23

Teamwork

Ronald Reagan once said, "There's no limit to what a man can do or where he can go if he doesn't mind who gets the credit." There are no solo players or stars on a team, and there is definitely no "I" in the word "team." Helping other team members to score and succeed is the mark of great players and leaders, and it is one of the fastest ways to catapult a department or a company to the next level. Unselfishness is the key to help other people grow, directly reflecting and impacting your own growth.

Love, the unselfish quality of wanting to help others, is the foundation to effective teambuilding. When you love, you trust, and when you trust, you bond. Nothing pulls a team closer together or builds loyalty better than love and trust.

A team is like a machine—each part is necessary and has to work properly for the entire operation to work efficiently. Each team is like a living organism, and each part is made up of the different gifts, talents, and personalities that God has given each member in order to work efficiently. Some of us are artistic, some logical and analytical, while others are social and outspoken. Some may be comfortable working in a quick-paced environment, but others work best at a slower pace. All team member styles and velocities are necessary for the team to work at the peak of productivity.

When you are part of a team, you share the credit—you don't strive for personal credit. A team member fully understands his role and the role of the other members of the team in relation to the "big picture" of the organization. There is no internal competition on a team because internal competition doesn't produce positive results for anyone.

Together You Accomplish More

The word "synergy" comes from the Greek *synergos*, which means working together. Synergism is a condition in which the total combined effort of a team is greater than the sum of the single efforts of individuals. Team performance is an unselfish attitude where you work together for the accomplishment of the end result, the goal, and not for your own glorification or self-gratification.

Teamwork involves the actions of a group of people who share a commitment of working together, relying on the interdependence of each team member to ensure the team's overall performance and accomplish or exceed set goals.

A team is an integral unit working toward organizational objectives and goals that will benefit the whole group, rather than an aggregate of individuals working selfishly on independent goals.

The following are a few of my favorite quotes on teamwork:

> *"Individual commitment to a group effort — that is what makes a team work, a company work, a society work, a civilization work."*
>
> - Vince Lombardi
> *American football coach*

> *"The leaders who work most effectively, it seems to me, never say "I." And that's not because they have trained themselves not to say "I," they just don't think "I." They think "we"; they think "team." They understand their job is to make the team function. They accept responsibility and don't sidestep it, but 'we' gets the credit ... . This is what creates trust, what enables you to get the task done."*
>
> - Peter F. Drucker

> *"In the end, all business operations can be reduced to three words: people, product and profits. Unless you've got a good team, you can't do much with the other two."*
>
> - Lee Iacocca

"No problem is insurmountable. With a little courage, teamwork and determination, a person can overcome anything."

- Unknown

'When a team outgrows individual performance and learns team confidence, excellence becomes a reality."

- Joe Paterno
American football coach

"Teamwork is so important that it is virtually impossible for you to reach the heights of your capabilities or make the money that you want without becoming very good at it."

- Brian Tracy
*Author. Lecturer,
and American television host*

It's not the style that motivates me, as much as an attitude of openness that I have when I go into a project.

— Herbie Hancock

Attribute 24

Effective Project Management

A true professional knows how to turn ideas into reality. Nothing happens until you execute. The ability to execute, which means to become a doer and not just a dreamer, is one of the most important and powerful skills a professional can possess. You must know how to properly execute in order to turn your dreams and visions into reality.

Project Execution

Execution can take the form of ideas, learned concepts and skills, business processes, customer service programs, and projects.

Project management is the process of planning, organizing, and managing tasks, individual duties that make up a project, and resources, such as money, time, or people, in order to accomplish a defined objective, usually within certain time constraints, resources, or costs.

In its basic form, a project plan can be as simple as a list of tasks with their start and finish dates written on a notepad. The plan can also be more elaborate with hundreds of tasks, resources, and a projected budget of millions of dollars.

The key to successful project implementation is the (1) breaking of the project into easy, more manageable tasks, (2) scheduling the tasks, (3) communicating with the team or people responsible for the execution of the various tasks, and (4) tracking, supervising, and controlling the tasks and cost as work progresses.

The three major factors that affect a project are:

1. *Time:* The time needed to complete the project, which is reflected in your project scheduling.

2. *Money:* The project budget, which is based on the cost of resources such as the people, equipment, and materials required to do the tasks.

3. *Scope:* The goals and tasks of the project and the work required to complete them.

Every time you adjust any of these elements, the other two will be affected.

The following outline describes the questions you must understand and answer for a successful project implementation process:

Why
   • Why are we doing this? What is the main objective
     and benefit?

Who
   • Who will do it?

What
   • What resources do I need to implement and organize
     this idea?
       - Money
       - Time
       - People
       - Equipment
       - Forms, software
       - Skills
       - Communication tools—memo, e-mail, verbal, story board

When

- When would be a realistic date to complete this project?

- When should each task be completed in order to complete the project on time?

Where

- What events need to take place and where should they happen?

- What activity needs to happen before other activities can take place?

How

- How many phases should there be, one or more?

- Outline the detailed tasks needed to complete a phase (a number of tasks completes a phase and a number of phases completes a project).

- How much will the project cost?

- How are you going to track the progress of the project?

- How, how often, and to whom will you report the progress of the project?

- How will you supervise and control the project in respect to budget, people's performance, progress according to the timeline, and quality?

Rules for Effective Project Management

1. Clearly define the project.
   - Decide how it looks, smells, sounds, feels, and tastes using the five-sensing technique introduced by Walt Disney

2. Set a clear project goal.
   - What is the ultimate outcome?

3. Define the project objectives.
   - What is the purpose, reason, strategies, and ideas to reach the goal?

4. Establish the activities necessary to complete each objective.

5. Establish the time schedule estimates, working it
   backwards from the date the project must be completed.

6. Determine the resources you wills need in each phase.

7. Plan your communications with people
   assigned to the project.

8. Empower the project team members to
   make decisions as well as mistakes.

9. Encourage risk-taking and creativity.

10. Track the progress and manage the schedule and budget.

11. Keep everyone connected and informed on the
    progress and changes of the project.

12. Manage your resources to make sure everyone is doing their
    job. Encourage them and find out if they need anything
    from you to complete their assigned responsibilities.

13. Manage the project scope and make adjustments as needed.

14. Manage the risks as they arise.

15. Report project status and progress to everyone involved.

16. Finally, always remember that *winners do what losers don't
    like to do*. Nothing happens until we execute, so just do it!

These bullet points are just guidelines to what you should know is involved in the effective management of projects. By no means am I intending to provide you with a "Sixteen Easy Steps to Manage a Project" guide. This chapter is intended to open your mind about the complexities of project management and show you how the foundation for success lies in the amount of detail you put in the *planning* process, as well as the overall assertive execution and supervision of the entire process, timeline, cost, and final outcome.

You must take personal responsibility. You cannot change the circumstances, the seasons or the wind, but you can change yourself. That is something you have charge of.

— Jim Rohn

American speaker and author
Famous for motivational audio programs
for business and life

Man must cease attributing his problems to his environment, and learn again to exercise his will — his personal responsibility in the realm of faith and morals.

— Albert Schweitzer

German medical missionary, theologian,
musician, and philosopher
1952 Nobel Peace Prize
(1875-1965)

Attribute 25

Taking Personal Responsibility

Personal responsibility is the acknowledgement that you are solely responsible for the consequences of your choices. There are no victims. You are responsible for what you choose to feel, think, or do. In fact, the only things in life we can control are our thoughts and actions.

Emotional maturity and professionalism is shown when we accept to choose the direction of our life and choose not to blame others or make up excuses for those choices. We must stop the defensive thoughts and rationalizations for why others are to blame for who we are, what we do, what has happened to us, or what we are going to become. We are the architect of our own circumstances. We are totally responsible for determining who we are and for choosing the choices that impact our life.

One of the most important lessons you will learn in life is to take responsibility and face the consequences of your actions.

Your attitude in life determines your feelings toward any events or actions that come your way, no matter how negative they seem to be. When you choose a positive attitude to deal with life, you start realizing you don't have to depend on others to make you feel good about yourself.

As you enter adulthood and maturity, you start determining how your self-esteem will develop, but only *if* you don't allow other people, circumstances, or the culture to define who you are. By refusing and ceasing to feel sorry for the "bad deal" you may have been handed by people in the past, and as you start taking responsibility for changing the direction of your own circumstances by changing your choices, you will find new direction and experience a new sense of significance in life.

We must recognize that we can choose our responses to people, circumstances, actions, and events in our life.

Likewise, when you let go of your need to take responsibility for the actions of others, whether it's to please or be pleasing to them, you will start feeling a tremendous sense of relief and freedom from this self-imposed burden. This choice will immediately and positively impact your health as well as your emotional well-being,

As for those people whose responsibilities you have consistently carried upon yourself by being an enabler or by consistently doing someone else's work, choosing to let them fly on their own can become a great opportunity for them to learn to take responsibility for their own lives and to start growing up emotionally.

Some of the people that have adversely affected your life in the past may have done so out of their own emotional, intellectual, or psychological limitations, their own hurtful background, or because of an overall lack of wisdom and ignorance. As you begin to accept this truth, and as you *forgive* and *let go* of blame and anger toward those in your past who fell short of your expectactions, you will be able to heal your anger, hostility, pessimism, and depression over past hurts, pains, abuse, mistreatment, and misdirection.

Forgiveness is a choice. Therefore, failure to accept personal responsibility for your own forgiveness in life will result in negative consequences, such as becoming overly dependent on others for recognition and approval, or becoming hostile or depressed over how unfairly you have been or are being treated.

If these emotions are left unchecked, you may become fearful about taking risks or making decisions, which can lead you down a road of failure. Accepting personal responsibility requires that we develop the ability to take risks in life and accept the consequences of these risks, no matter if they are positive or negative.

People can also become unsuccessful in personal relationships if they become emotionally or physically inbalanced. This happens because they choose and accept the thought that they don't have any control or responibilty over their destiny. This thought-choice can lead to hopelesness, which can lead to addictions such as alcohol, drugs, food, gambling, compulsive shopping, sex, smoking, or overworking. All these behaviors can happen as a result of taking control of your life in the wrong way.

People who have the bad habit of not accepting personal responsibility are seen by others as immature, incompetent, and unworthy of respect, because they go through life blaming people, circumstances, and their past environment for the outcomes of their own actions.

Make a conscious decision to let go of anger, fear, blame, mistrust, and insecurity. The best way to let go successfully is to review your spiritual beliefs and to review your personal relationship with God.

If you feel that you are struggling with deflecting personal responsibility, seek out and accept professional help for yourself. This is a sign of strength, not of weakness. It is essential that you take off the masks of pretensions and behavioral patterns and start realizing that you are solely in charge and responsible for the direction your life takes.

To help overcome your fears, rebut irrational beliefs and make constant positive affirmations about yourself and your ability to own and manage the consequences of your actions. Recognize and embrace that you are the master of the choices that you make.

" Rudeness is the weak man's imitation of strength. "

— Jim Rohn
American writer
1902-1983

" A little rudeness and disrespect can elevate a

meaningless interaction to a battle of wills and add

drama to an otherwise dull day. "

— Bill Watterson
American author of the comic strip
Calvin & Hobbes, b.1958

Attribute 26

Avoiding Rude Behavior

Rudeness is defined as lacking social refinement. The message behind rudeness is one of ignorance and indifference toward good social manners and intentional discourtesy. It is a message of self-centeredness and selfishness. It reflects a lack of polish and gentleness.

Rudeness is shown by word, action and inaction. Rudeness of word is when we are verbally unpolished, curse, use street or offensive language, tell untasteful jokes, speak too personally in conversations with people we don't have an intimate relationship with, use vulgar language, express attitude, talk at the same time others are talking, constantly interrupt conversations, or talk in a loud voice tone.

Inaction rudeness includes those actions and demeanors that disrespect and diminish people, such as being abrupt and/or "in your face," not being courteous, ignoring people's feelings and concerns, impoliteness, or lack of civility.

Rudeness of inaction includes those behaviors of omission, which send a rude message to people without using words. It's more about what you don't do than what you do. Behaviors such as not returning phone calls (including sales calls), not paying attention to people when they are talking, ignoring people ("cold shoulder treatment"), being inconsiderate and uncaring, and acting apathetic are all examples of how you can be rude without using words.

Rudeness turns people off at the speed of a bullet. The following is a list of rude behaviors to avoid at all costs if you want to win the respect of others:

- Not returning phone calls or messages.

- Answering your cell phone or checking messages in the middle of a conversation.

- Reading or replying to text messages or taking cell phone calls in the middle of a conversation, a business meeting, or a luncheon.

- Flossing in public.

- Talking loudly on the cell phone while in public.

- Using bad language.

- Using slang terms like "B.S." and "Freaking."

- Yawning without covering your mouth.

- Yawning in the middle of a meeting.

- Talking with your mouth full of food.

- "Me first" aggressive actions.

- Burping in public.

- Typing on the computer while talking with someone on the phone.

- Interrupting others when they speak.

- Beginning e-mails without a "hello" or "good morning" greeting.

- Not sending a "Thank You" note when someone has done something for you.

- Not acknowledging receipt of a gift, package, letter, etc. that has been sent to you.

- Misspelling words in your e-mail communications.

- All selfish behavior.

- Indifference in customer assistance, such as not making eye contact.

- Aggressive driving.

- Being frequently late to appointments and meetings.

- Chewing gum in a professional environment.

- Not looking directly and attentively at the speaker while in a conversation.

- Filing or clipping nails while in a meeting.

Peace is not absence of conflict; it is the ability to handle conflict by peaceful means.

— Ronald Reagan
American 40th US president (1981- 89
(1911-2004)

Attribute 27

Conflict Resolution

Webster's dictionary defines conflict as: *(a) competitive or opposing action of incompatibles: antagonistic state or action (as of divergent ideas, interests, or persons) (b): mental struggle resulting from incompatible or opposing needs, drives, wishes, or external or internal demands.*

Conflict has to do with the way individuals handle grievances, clashes in opinions, and right and wrong judgments. Conflict resolution is the process of resolving a dispute, a difference, or a disagreement.

The process of conflict resolution doesn't need to be contentious or aggressive. On the contrary, the best resolutions are the ones that are handled in a civil, non-aggressive "brain storming" style.

One of the most effective techniques for conflict resolution is when you discover and unselfishly share information about another's needs, perceptions, and values through a creative thinking process that adequately addresses each party's interests, resulting in the satisfaction of both parties.

For this process to work, each party must come to the table with honesty, transparency, and without the attitude of taking advantage of the information provided by other parties in order to achieve one-sided gains. The process should be totally focused on coming up with creative solutions that will solve each party's needs and must be completely unemotional.

The following is a summary of the process to conflict resolution:

1. Write a brief list with a description of the issues you want to resolve so you can gain understanding of what you want, why you want it, and how it affects you if you don't have it. For example, if you want the other party to stop a certain behavior, you must start by clearly defining what behavior you want the other person to stop doing. Then explain why or how you feel each time the person repeats the behavior, and, finally, how the behavior affects you personally.

2. Mutually share information with the other party in order to fully gain understanding of the content (issues and needs) and the intent (feelings and intentions) of each other.

3. Both parties should ask as many questions as possible in order to gain understanding of each other's needs.

4. Start a creative thinking session, verbalizing and writing down every idea that comes to your mind without rationalizing or making judgments of the idea. The more ideas you come up with from "gut feelings" the better. Usually the instinctive or "gut" thinking ends up being the best idea.

5. Take control of your emotions. This is a process designed to come up with solutions and to harmonize each other's needs, not to think selfishly or to "score" points to get what you want. Keep in mind that this is not an adversarial process, but a creative thinking process. It is an unselfish, understanding-gaining, and solution-oriented process—not an egocentric one.

6. Separate ego from the issues. This process is not about you personally, but about solving the issues and needs of the group.

7. Use a conversational style during the process by incorporating humor, analogies, acceptance, and understanding language. Ask for clarification (respond), rather than jumping into emotional conclusions (reacting).

8. Choose the best ideas and create a consensus about which idea or combination of ideas best meet each other's needs. Now is the time to rationalize, analyze, and reduce the ideas to the ones that best meet each other's needs.

9. Build mutually beneficial agreements. After coming up with a final list of ideas, write them down with specific instructions on how to implement the ideas, as well as the necessary resources and alloted time frame.

10. You may have to initiate another creative thinking exercise to come up with specific ways to implement the ideas.

11. Generate options or alternate plans in case the original ideas to be implemented don't work according to expectations. This method forces you to think in different directions. Make sure that you remain flexible, considering all options and setting realistic expectations.

" Knowledge is power when it comes to boundaries. Those who do not know the boundaries are destined to cross them. People have been eaten for doing so! "

— Unknown

Attribute 28

Personal and Professional Boundaries

Learning about boundaries in your personal and business relationships is of the utmost importance, because boundaries allow you to know when you will cause offense to someone and when someone offends you or disrespects your desires. Boundaries allow you to have your own personal space and rules of engagement. You may feel angry when someone crosses your relationship boundary because you may feel threatened, frustrated, violated, or hurt.

Therefore, establishing healthy boundaries for yourself and the people you deal with allows your relationships to be constructive, functional, respectful, and balanced.

Boundaries are about knowing how to have healthy relationships and interactions with others by respecting their desires. In an employment situation, most employees know that stealing from the company is grounds for ending the employment relationship. Crossing the "honesty boundary" through theft can cause termination of employment. Crossing other relationship boundaries can bring about consequences that are just as damaging.

The following points will help you in beginning to set healthy personal boundaries:

1. Make a written decisive list of what you want and don't
    want people to do or say to you. A good idea is to classify the
    boundaries as (a) general boundaries and (b) boundaries

for specific people, types of relationships, or circumstances. The boundaries you need to work on with other people will be revealed to you as you think of those things that frustrate, anger, or hurt you the most. Memorize this list and make them part of your value-system.

2. If you feel one of your boundaries has been violated, educate or inform the person (in a matter-of-fact way) of what they are doing that crosses over your set boundaries. Just inform them how the violation affects you personally. Be constructive about communicating and enforcing your limits. Tell them specifically, what you want and don't want, like or don't like, as well as communicate how you feel about it.

3. Decide the consequences of each violation. If the violation persists after educating them the first time, warn them about what you are determined to do next time the violation occurs. Consequences may include a temporary separation ("Next time I will walk away until you cool off" or "If this doesn't stop right now, I will take this matter to your boss"). Depending on the seriousness of the violation, it may be necessary to distance yourself from the person permanently. Most importantly, you must be willing, ready ,and determined to enforce the consequences that are a result of the violation.

At the beginning, particularly for the people who've been in your life and have lived under your old boundary-less life, your new boundaries may be hard on them. They may overreact by counter-attacking, possibly retaliating by guilt tripping you ("After all I have done for you...") or using other manipulation tactics. Remember, change is difficult for most people.

The key is to be as matter-of-fact, emotionless, and straightforward as possible when you are defining and setting your limits, likes, and dislikes with them.

Boundaries in Business

The following information will help you in starting to set boundaries in business and professional settings:

Sexual Harassment

Behavior that may, at first, start as a joke becomes sexual harassment when it is (1) unwelcome (by either men or women), (2) becomes persistent, or (3) creates a hostile, unfriendly, or intimidating environment. Such behavior could be verbal, nonverbal, or physical.

Make a strong commitment to never cross the boundary of sexual harassment in any of its manifestations. Not only could you be personally exposing yourself as a sexual harasser, but you will also be exposing your company to a lawsuit. If that isn't enough,you will, more than likely, be fired.

Friendships in the Workplace

Many people in the workplace confuse being friendly with being personal friends. Being friendly and amicable only implies a disposition to live on good terms and harmony with others and of being helpful.

On the other hand, friendships you develop at work are fundamentally different from personal friendships. A job provides financial security, If forced to choose between keeping your source of income and a friendship, most people would choose to keep their job. You have a lot more at stake when choosing to enter into a workplace friendship.

The right group of friends can be a great influence on your career, but the wrong group can get you fired. A true professional recognizes the difference between being friendly and thinking that someone is their buddy because they are civil and friendly. They also know that crossing this boundary may be fatal to their career.

Monster.com provides the following advice:

- Be discreet about your friend's confidences, and think carefully about the type of information you choose to divulge.

- If you think your friendship puts you or your friend in a compromising position on the job, talk about it. If necessary, withdraw yourself from situations that might be a conflict of interest.

- Find out if your company has a policy regarding workplace friendships and follow the rules.

Abusive Behaviors

The first sign of an abusive situation is when one person relinquishes control over the other.

- *Those Who Control Through Criticism*
    - People who make other people feel like they never do anything right—nothing is ever good enough.
    - An attitude that their way is the only right way.

- *Those Who Control Through Moodiness and Angry Threats*
    - People that expect other people to read their minds and lose their temper when others cannot do so.
    - When people give others the "silent treatment," expecting them to have the ability to figure out what they have done wrong and how to fix it.

- *Those Who Control Through Denying Your Perceptions*
    - When people act very cruelly and then say you are too sensitive and cannot take a joke.
    - People that often break promises and then claim to have never made the promise.

- *Those Who Control by Ignoring Our Needs and Opinions*
    - People that act like others' opinions are not important, are stupid, or not welcomed.

- *Those Who Control Through Decision Making*
    - Bosses who want to make all the decisions and don't empower other people to make decisions or take risks.

- *Those Who Control Through Money*
    - When bosses manipulate and control by threatening not to give you a raise if you don't comply, or make sure to remind you that the reason why you are eating is because of the money they provide for you.

- *Those Who Control Through Shifting Responsibility*
    - Always blaming others for everything that happens and never taking personal responsibility for anything.

- *Those Who Control Through Gossip*
    - Some people feel powerful as information brokers. They want to let everyone know that they are "in the loop" on everything

that's happening around the workplace, and they thrive by doing this.

• Rumors can be incredibly disruptive and destructive within an organization. A lack of information or the wrong information can get rumors started, contrary to forthright or honest explanations, which will usually stop them.

• It is important that as a professional you recognize and clearly differentiate between information sharing and gossip. It's also important that you immediately separate yourself from it and choose not to participate when you hear it. First and foremost, don't repeat what you hear.

Violent or Threatening Behavior

Workplace violence, verbal or physical, that includes threats or actual abuse only escalates with time and is never excusable. Never permit anyone to abuse you verbally. This is a boundary that no one should ever cross in the workplace. However, if they do, you should, in no uncertain terms, tell them that their behavior is not acceptable and what the consequences will be the next time they cross the line.

If you think this couldn't happen in your company, think again. It's estimated by the Occupational Safety and Health Administration (OSHA) that two million Americans are victims of workplace violence annually.

Dishonesty and Theft

Dishonesty and theft include the following: the theft of time, office supplies, and the use of office equipment for personal projects without permission, lying or calling in sick to take a day off, taking petty cash money for personal use, falsifying or padding expense reports, and using the company's computer for sending personal e-mails or surfing the Web.

Security experts say that as many as 30% of workers steal, resulting in an estimated loss of $50 billion a year from U.S. companies, thus contributing to as many as one-third of business bankruptcies.

Substance Abuse

Substance abuse is more widespread than most employers realize. The U.S. Department of Health and Human Services estimates that 6–11% of adults are substance abusers. Substance abuse costs U.S. employers an estimated $100 billion a year. Illegal drugs have led financially desperate employees to commit fraud and exhibit violent behavior in the workplace.

Never hire or promote in your own image. It is foolish to replicate your strength and idiotic to replicate your weakness. It is essential to employ, trust, and reward those whose perspective, ability, and judgment are radically different from yours.

— Unknown

Attribute 29

Getting Hired

I find it amazing how many job candidates act as if they are not really interested in being hired. With the advent and increased popularity of online recruitment, this attitude, as well as the lack of professionalism, has been increasing exponentially.

Recently, our company had three openings for high-level sales position. Upon calling the candidates for an interview, I was baffled at the amount of candidates who asked us what position we were calling about. I call these types of candidates "resume spammers," or "fishers." They blindly send a barrage of resumes without any thought or particular consideration, expecting an employer to take the bait and call them...absurd!

On another occasion, one candidate asked me for the link to the recruitment ad we posted, which was on one of the most popular online job search sites... incredible!

A candidate that doesn't even know or keep track of the companies they have applied to shows a perception of apathy, arrogance, lack of professionalism and preparation, ignorance, laziness, and denotes a measure of immaturity.

When looking for a job:

- **Get organized** — Keep a list of every company you have applied to, the date you applied, the name of the position, and kind of industry. Keep detailed records handy for when you receive a call, so you don't get caught off balance.

- **Read the ad twice and carefully** — Know exactly what skills and attributes the ad is asking for. Don't send a resume to companies when you have only read the headline and first paragraph of the recruitment ad. Show self-respect and respect for others by studying the ad and understanding the requirements of the position before sending your resume.

- **Show interest and enthusiasm** — You will never have a second chance for a good first impression. When you answer a recruitment call, sound energetic, positive, eager, interested, and grateful. Remember that your attitude will determine your altitude.

- **Always include an introduction or cover letter** — A resume shows your skills and experience, but a cover letter shows your attitude. Take the time to write a well composed letter that reflects who you are and what it is that you will bring to the table of the organization. This may be your only opportunity to show your value.

- **If you can't make an interview appointment, call** — Never stand up an employer; this is a smaller world than you may think. Not canceling an appointment or showing up late is the psychological equivalent of the childish expression "whatever," which denotes apathy, carelessness, disrespect, and immaturity. You will never get a decent job reflecting that kind of attitude.

- **Don't rush to ask about the compensation package** — Show that you respect your time and theirs. If the salary or compensation package is the first thing you're interested in, it becomes a mute point if you don't get past the first interview. Asking for money early on in the interview process, especially before you have the chance to show what it is that the potential new employer will be paying for, shows a selfish, money-focused, "taker" attitude. Focus on showing the prospective employer what you can contribute and how you can add value to their organization.

- **Don't interview the interviewer** — Don't ask questions early in the interview unless they ask you if you have any questions. Don't confuse the roles; the employer is the *interviewer* and you are the *interviewed* candidate. You will be perceived as rude, manipulative, and as if you are trying to take control of the interview, especially in the first interview.

- **Make it short and to the point** — Listen attentively to the employer and their questions. Give short and concise answers to their questions. Don't go on tangents and give personal commentary. Listen to the intent (what they mean), as well as the content (the subject or issue) of their questions. Listening with intensity, understanding the intent and content of the speaker, and responding accordingly are the foundations of effective communication.

- **Research, research, research** — Study the company and the industry of your prospective employer so you can talk with intelligence and show that you know how to do your homework. By showing a basic knowledge of your future employer and their industry, you come across as a true professional who is interested in taking the time to get to know them and has a foundational understanding of them.

- **Strengths and weaknesses** — Understand what your strengths and weaknesses are, personal and professional, and don't be afraid to honestly and humbly verbalize them in a short sentence. Also be prepared to express what you are doing to strengthen your weaknesses. This shows humility, strength of character, and self-knowledge.

- **Follow every interview with a handwritten "thank you" note** — Stress to your prospective employer again that, if hired, you will be do your best, and briefly state just a few of your attitude attributes that make you the right candidate for the job.

- **Come to all interviews looking "like the President"** — Don't underestimate the importance of looking professional and conservative. Unless you are applying for a position in an industry where casual dress is appropriate and expected, wear business-like dress to an interview. It's always good to err on the side of professionalism.

- **Follow up** — To obtain an interview, be persistent, but not a pest. Call to find out if they received your resume, to let them know that you are looking forward to an interview because your qualifications perfectly match the requirements of the position, to ask if the position has already been filled, or to let them know that you are still available and interested in the position.

- **Don't criticize your previous employers** — This is a major mistake because it shows disloyalty and presents you as a disgruntled employee and a gossip. If you don't have something positive to say about your former employers, say very little.

- **Be friendly, but not too familiar** — Show respect, professionalism, a friendly demeanor, flexibility, eagerness, optimism, and true interest in the position. On one occasion, a candidate that I was interviewing for the first time called me "buddy" over the phone. That was the moment he automatically disqualified himself for the position.

" The human being who lives only for himself finally reaps nothing but unhappiness. Selfishness corrodes. Unselfishness ennobles, satisfies. Don't put off the joy derivable from doing helpful, kindly things for others. "

— B. C. Forbes
*Scottish-born American editor and founder
of Forbes Magazine (1917) 1880-1954*

Attribute 30

Let's Talk About Our Identity

Have you ever asked yourself why you are on planet Earth, who you are, or why you exist? Have you tried desperately to fit in in order to be accepted, respected, and loved? We all struggle at one time or another with the issue of needing significance in life — *the search for meaning and purpose.*

All too often we permit society, Hollywood, the culture, and other people to define our happiness or who we are through their belief that having a certain car, drinking certain beer, living in a certain neighborhood, having a certain title, wearing a certain fashion, or buying a certain product will define who we are and/or make us happy.

In our consumer driven society of instant gratification and false significance, we often struggle with buying things we don't need with money we haven't earned in order to impress people we don't know, which brings us debt we can't pay off.

In a world where we are constantly competing with others by keeping score based on what we have, our social status, titles, etc., we have lost our perspective of what's really important in life. Many of us are greatly confused between quality of living, which is defined by the things we have, and quality of life, which is defined by the values that determine who we really are.

Many of us have tried many ways to fulfill this craving for significance: drugs and alcohol, sex, titles, success and achievement, overworking, sports, luxury cars, material things, wealth, popularity and fame, and other self-gratifying behaviors. In fact, the great paradox is that many things that start as fun or pleasurable actually result in a life of pain, divorce, financial disaster, disease, addictions, and relationship problems. The dilemma lies in that significance is not possible unless our actions contribute to the well-being and greater good of others.

True significance is not about what you do to feel better about yourself or impress others. Rather it is about what you do to help others and what you do for the benefit of humanity or your community. This truth is expressed by all major religions, but it is sadly the most overlooked principle in life. The core of significance in life is rooted in your motives and your attitudes toward others, in what you believe, as well as in your unselfish actions.

It is very important to analyze who you are and what is important in life before you set goals. You need to learn what you identify with before you are able to look for direction through life goals. In order to reach goals with peace of mind and joy in life, you need to find goals that are consistent with who you are, taking into consideration the common good.

You cannot force yourself to perform in a way that is not aligned with who you are. Failure in this area will bring disharmony, confusion, depression, friction, anger, lack of motivation, chronic frustration, and feelings of failure.

Many times we get so tangled and distracted in running the rat race that we don't seem to find time to examine our lives to gain understanding and definition of the things that are really important in life to us—not to anyone else, but to us.

In Rick Warren's book, *The Purpose Driven Life*, which has sold over 23 million copies and was listed as the #1 book on the New York Times Best Sellers list for weeks, he outlines five different values to bring purpose to your life based on spiritual values, not cultural values.

Paraphrasing Warren's insight and the Bible as the source of those insights, he points out that:

1. ***You were created for God's pleasure***, so the first purpose is to get to know who God is and to have a personal relationship of love with Him. To know God is to love Him. When you know God, you will start defining yourself based

on who God says you are, rather than on who society, your parents, or the culture says you are or should be.

2. ***You were created as part of God's family***, so your second purpose is to enjoy true and more significant friendships with the people God has placed in your life.

3. ***You were created to model the Jesus of the Bible***, which means to grow spiritually and become selfless (which is a lifelong process). Learn how to look for other people's good, rather than looking for self-gratification and thinking only in terms of "what's in it for me."

4. ***You were created to serve God***, so your fourth purpose is to love your neighbor with actions of love. True love is not a feeling, but a deliberate action you choose to take that benefits other people even when you don't feel like it. It is a choice, not a feeling.

5. ***You were created for a mission***, your ultimate mission in life. Once you become friends with God and you start enjoying the benefits of true significance, your mision is to encourage other people to search for significance by sharing with them where you are now as a result of your newly found friendship with God. Sharing the gift that God gave you with others, the gift of His friendship and true significance, becomes your mission in life and directs you to act lovingly towards others.

Don't confuse your purpose in life with being religious or the lacking desire for material goals and possessions—it has nothing to do with that. A goal is what you do, while a purpose is why you do what you do, also known as your motives. You can choose material possessions for self-gratification or you can choose to have the same material possessions for the benefit of sharing with others. The motives of why you want the possessions determine your true purpose in life.

You can choose to perform your job with the attitude of "I deserve better" or the belief that others are taking advantage of you. With this attitude you hear yourself saying, "I'm not getting paid what I deserve," or "I work for a bunch of jerks."

This attitude, however, will not bring you success in life or the workplace. Instead, choose to be the best that you can be, realizing that God didn't make you a mediocre person. You must be conscious and fully aware that you are an important member of a team. You must also be conscious that what you do in excellence helps other people in your department and, ultimately, in your organization.

The secret of job contentment is not in the circumstances, but in your attitude, despite the circumstances. Your attitude will determine your altitude in life and in the workplace. You are the only one who can choose whether you will be a victim or a conqueror.

Most people have confused ideas of what their priorities in life should be. In many cases, we live by the priorities others have set for us, instead of the priorities we have set for ourselves. The following list of priorities is in alignment with what most religions and great unselfish thinkers have taught us are top priorities in life:

> ***Priority #1:*** Getting to know and love God (through the study of God, sharing, praying, meditation, and living with an attitude of gratitude toward God).

> ***Priority #2:*** Family life, friends, and family values (experience the love of God through your family and friends).

> ***Priority #3:*** Helping and serving others (be good to others simply because God has been good to you).

> ***Priority #4:*** Work (with a positive attitude of gratitude).

> ***Priority #5:*** Rest (recharge your batteries for the next day).

When any of these priorities are out of balance or out of order, sooner or later you will experience moral, financial, family, or relational bankruptcy. A balanced set of priorities through a committed relationship with your Creator will bring to your life love, joy, peace, patience, kindness, goodness, faithfulness, gentleness, and self-control, which are all characteristics of a true professional.

If you have integrity, nothing else matters. If you don't have integrity, nothing else matters.

— Alan K. Simpson

You are in integrity when the life you are living on the outside matches who you are on the inside.

— Alan Cohen

Attribute 31

*Integrity: Acting What
You Believe*

You can't behave in a way that is contrary to what you believe, therefore, what you believe controls your behavior. Your life philosophy drives and controls your vision, passions, and actions.

In this chapter we are going to discuss two major philosophical issues in the life of a professional: business ethics and the impact of your spiritual life on your professional life (whether you believe in a Higher Power or not).

I have always admired the ethics of some of the old tycoons that have shaped our modern society. Inspired in the work of James D. Newton and based on his highly-recommended book *Uncommon Friends*, which is published by Harcourt Brace & Co., I would like to focus on and review the faith and life philosophies of five geniuses who were close friends: Henry Ford, Thomas Alva Edison, Harvey Firestone, Charles Lindberg. and Dr. Alexis Carrel, who was the 1912 Nobel Prize winner for his work on the suturing of blood vessels and organ transplants.

When these five friends got together, they loved to talk about the common good, industry, spirituality, the purpose of life, and many other principled and philosophical subjects that nourished their curiosity and intellect.

Henry Ford thought the purpose of making money was to help society as a whole and to provide service excellently and unselfishly. He said, *"The purpose of money is to provide more opportunity to perform more* service. Short-sighted businessmen think first of money, but service is what really makes or breaks businesses; without it, customers soon go somewhere else."

Ford goes on to say, "If money is your only hope for independence, you will never have it. It's our first duty to do the right thing, and this will earn us the right money." Isn't that a great principled statement?

An outstanding testimony on Henry Ford's character was written in a letter by Charles A. Lindbergh to Ford in June 1942. Lindbergh wrote, "You combine the characteristics that I admire most in men: success with humility, firmness with tolerance, and science with religion. Possibly the thing I admire the most about you is that you have built one of the world's greatest industries without letting it change your own outlook and character." This is one of the greatest character tributes and evidences of respect a man can ever expect to receive.

Thomas Alva Edison is well known in history, not only for his genius, perseverance, and character, but for his long, relentless hours of hard work. One of his statements that shows this attribute reads, "All things come to him who hustles while he waits."

Edison is also the best example of working for the needs of people and not for his own selfish purposes. He made the following statement to James D. Newton: "The secret of staying afloat is to create something that people will pay for. I didn't work at inventions unless I saw a market demand for them. I wasn't interested in making money as much as in being the first to invent something society needed. But if you do that, the money comes in."

As someone who worked selflessly, Edison's first concern wasn't about making money, but in bettering the lives of others: "What really interests me is inventing things the world needs."

Some quotes that define the depth of character and leadership skills of Harvey Firestone are as follows:

"Never be bullied into silence. Never allow yourself to be made a victim. Accept no one's definition of your life, but define yourself."

"The growth and development of people is the highest calling of leadership."

"Capital isn't that important in business. Experience isn't that important. You can get both of these things. What is important is ideas."

"You get the best out of others when you give the best of yourself."

"The secret of my success is a two word answer: Know people."

In a similarly principled statement, Charles Lindbergh said, *"We should see people as more important than things, the producer as more important than the product, peace of heart as more important than the prize of possession. That's what I believe as the balance of spirit, mind, and body."*

How were Ford, Lindbergh, Edison, Firestone, and even Carrel able to see past the human condition and serve selflessly? These great men were committed to moral principles and the greater good of society as a whole because they understood the source of all good in humanity was God. Their faith in God was public and a witness of everything that was right and good in them.

Lindbergh comments directly to a higher power, saying, *"When I'm flying, I'm a materialist — until I get my feet on the ground. When a flyer runs into something beyond the control of his own mind and body, he realizes very quickly that he's in the hands of an unseen power."*

In a memorable statement on commitment, he also said, *"It comes down to this: I have found that when you make a deep commitment (to God), unforeseen forces come to your aid. Getting to the point of deciding is the hard part. Once you are there, it is simple; we experience a spiritual rebirth."* This means that once we make a deep commitment, "something" gives us the power to resist what is contrary to our commitment.

Going further, Lindbergh defined the difference between internal surrender, which is humility, and external self-sacrifice, which is pride. Internal submission to a Higher Authority to guide us and to take care of our lives and decisions brings humility, a desirable character attribute. On the other hand, those things that we do to feel better about ourselves, (external self-sacrifice) or those things that we do for other people to notice us, fosters pride and selfishness, which is an undesirable character trait.

Lindbergh's wife, Anne, added to his statement that the most important commitment in life is to crucify our pride: *"...a commitment to relinquish as much of your will as you understand your Creator; to the degree you know Him or recognize Him or trust Him, or whatever."*

She said that if we don't believe in God, then you can perform an experiment. Ask God, *"If you are real, make it clear what it is I should do in life."* What is the result of the experiment? She said, *"He will do exactly that; He will show you the steps you should take."*

If you decide to conduct this experiment, don't expect bells and whistles to ring. But if tonight you make the decision to let God take control of your life with a sincere heart, positive expectations, and genuine contrition for your past deeds, tomorrow morning you will know that He is there. The decision to put your life in the hands of God, to trust him and follow Him, will have an extraordinary effect in your life. It will have the the same impact on your life as it had in the lives of these great men, who were so unashamedly to proclaim their faith in public.

Lindbergh recalls the first time he prayed for God to take control of his life in this statement: *"I have my ideals, but I can't live up to them. I don't have what it takes. Okay, I've loused things up — if you are there and can call the shots, here is my will and my life. You run it, you fly it."* From that moment on, Lindbergh said he gained a spiritual insight and a sense of direction in life like he had never known before.

In response to his wife's experiment, Dr. Alexis Carrel told Ford, *"Henry, it is not a question of trying to persuade your intellect that God exists. Instead, try sitting quietly and just suppose God is there. Listen and see what thoughts come into your mind. In other words, let your intuition reveal truth to you. The thoughts that come might not be so much about God, but about us."*

Carrel's advice for Ford came from his belief that God, as an infinite being, is a difficult concept for the finite mind: "There is a power in the universe beyond man's intellectual grasp."

Dr. Alexis Carrel, in conversation with his friends, shared with them the following statement: *"Man does not live by bread alone (Luke 4:4); nor does society. Men need to keep equilibrium between material and spiritual nourishment."* He added, *"The point is to concentrate your attention on something beyond the self; then comes inner peace. The inner control only emerges from the acceptance of values such as love, honesty, purity of motive, and regard for others."*

He believed that men had become isolated as self-sufficient, independent beings. Through this isolation, Carrel believed that men had made a mess out of the resources of the planet and, ultimately, of their own lives. He thought that men had lost their identities and purpose in life, thinking that the world and life revolved around the indiviual, and that they had forgotten they are surrounded by scores of people who impact each other's lives with their actions, for better or worse.

The purpose of this chapter is to show you, the aspiring professional, that your profession is not a separation from your faith. After World War II, Lindbergh toured a concetration camp, and he became puzzled how people who accomplish brilliant scientific experiments could live in a world alongside those who degrade and deprive their fellow people: *"Why have we allowed our pursuit of science and power to pervert the human spirit?"*

Indeed, our post-modern society has allowed and promoted science as something incompatible with God, instead of as the way to understand how God's creation works. But what amazed and intrigued me the most when I read Uncommon Friends is that these illustrious pioneers of science and industry talked freely and publicly about their faith as the fundamental nature of who they were. Lindbergh, Firestone, Edison, Carrel, and Ford all understood that their faith in God was what provided them success in their fields, not money or anything else that promotes the self. Instead of separating their faith from their profession, they combined them, thus creating success.

In today's materialistic culture it has become unfashionable and politically incorrect to talk about faith or God. But it is our faith in God that brings meaning and direction to an otherwise senseless world. On our own, we don't have the power to follow any kind of moral code, but in God we have all the power and morality we need to live a pure and joyful life.

Most of our founding fathers were God-revering people. These brilliant minds and courageous men include: Alexander Hamilton (signer of the Constitution), Daniel Boone (Revolutionary Officer and Legislator), Daniel Webster (Statesman and cousin to the creator of Webster's Dictionary), George Washington (first U.S. President), James Madison (former U.S. President), John Adams (former U.S. President), John Marshall (Chief Justice of the U.S. Supreme Court and Secretary Of State), Patrick Henry (Founding Father), Samuel Adams (signer of the Declaration). All of these were great men who believed in the Almighty and lived by faith and submission to God, unapologetically.

How, then, can our relationship with God now be considered as intolerant, closed minded, or out of style? Are we becoming smarter than our Founding Fathers, greatest industrialists, and most brilliant minds, or are we just becoming more proud and self-centered?

" Your legacy is the life you live and then leave behind. It includes everything you've ever done ... and not done. "

— Brian Mast
Author, business owner, and father

Attribute 32

Life Values and Legacy

Your core beliefs in life shape your value system. Your belief system consists of rooted assumptions (those things you have been trained to believe from childhood), cultural values (those things that you like and embrace from your cultural system), doctrinal values (those lessons about life, religion, politics, and ideology that establish your judgment of right and wrong), and aesthetic values (your conclusions about what is beautiful, ugly, pleasant, or unpleasant to your eyes).

You can value materialism and selfishness, or you can value spiritualism, love, and unselfishness. Your quality of life and legacy will be the sum total of your choices and value system in life.

The original purpose of this book, which is to preserve the original definition of professionalism as a character trait, is one that impacts and determines your legacy.

Allow me to review some of the previous segments of this book:

- *Be reliable*
- *Learning is never over for the professional*
- *Attitude*
- *Discipline*
- *Self-Control*
- *Temperance*
- *Unselfishness*

- *Ability to train and delegate*
- *Leadership by example*
- *Attitude of excellence*
- *Teamwork*
- *Taking personal responsibility*
- *Start with identity*
- *Integrity*
- *Legacy*

This is an effective list of tips, secrets, patterns, and habits that will greatly help anyone who masters them. The combination of all of these character traits reflects upon you as a business person, a professional, and an individual.

Each of these character traits, when taken seriously and turned into action, will produce positive attitudes, success in business (with peace), and the legacy of a life driven by purpose—to sow seeds unselfishnessly and with goodness.

Your belief system, your attitude, and your actions will determine if those seeds will continue to spread and grow in the lives of the people you have touched and for future generations after you are gone.

Intentionally leaving a legacy is too important for anyone to ignore. Your legacy is undoubtedly about leaving an unforgettable mark that will impact the lives of others; it is about how many people you have touched in this life with your kindness, mentoring, and love. No one will remember the balance of your bank account after you die, except for those who will keep and enjoy your money when you are gone. On the contrary, the people you have touched in this life will keep impacting other people, which is the real purpose-driven meaning of life.

The legacy we leave to our children will speak of the life we have lived on this earth, and it will speak volumes of the life we are choosing to lead now.

Therefore, leave a legacy that will speak honorably of your life and character for future generations. *Create a legacy of purpose that reflects the wisdom, love, and beauty of God on Earth!*

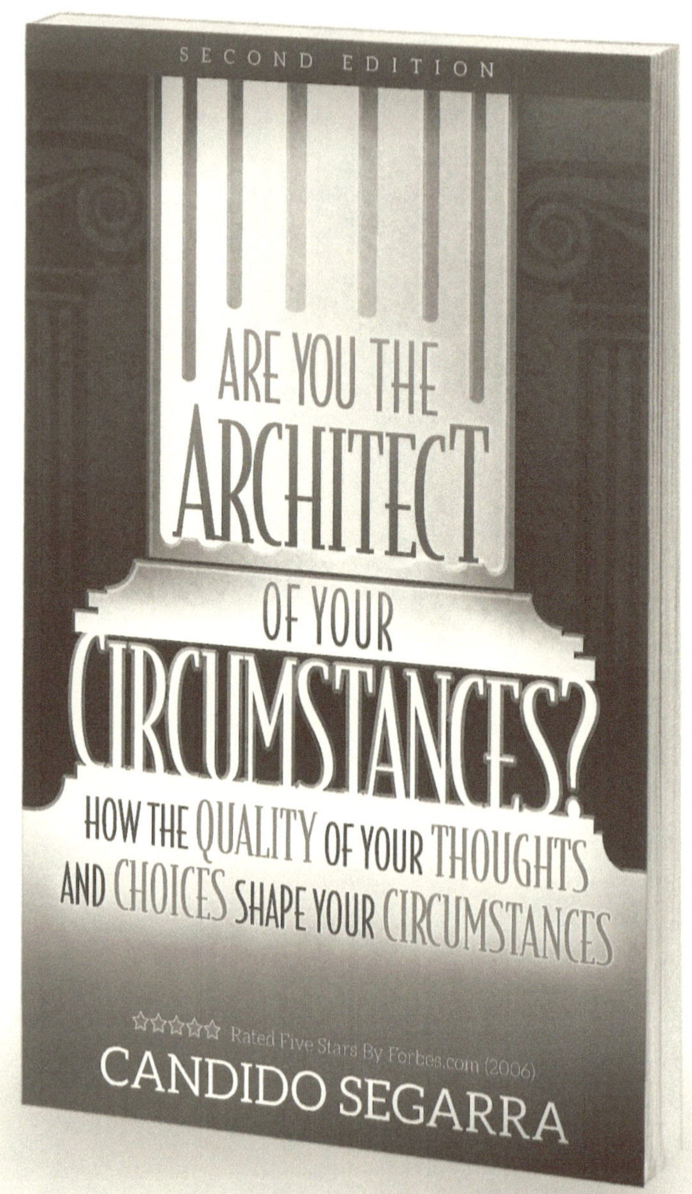
SECOND EDITION
ARE YOU THE ARCHITECT
OF YOUR
CIRCUMSTANCES?
HOW THE QUALITY OF YOUR THOUGHTS
AND CHOICES SHAPE YOUR CIRCUMSTANCES
Rated Five Stars By Forbes.com (2006)
CANDIDO SEGARRA

Testimonials

Are You the Architect of Your Circumstances?

Forbes® **Book Reviews:**

★★★★★ *"Excellent book with great information that is written in a concise manner that requires the reader to think. It could change your life in the most positive way."*

amazon.com **Book Reviews:**

★★★★★ ***Renew your mind!,***
This book takes no time to get down to the nitty-gritty and changes your perspective on circumstance. Our thought life really is more significant than we make it out to be and we ought to be more aware of its outpouring into our daily lives.

Candido's sincerity in this book proposes a certain clarity that is difficult to find in other philosophical and theological publications. Although it is a short read it offers a lot to chew on. I recommend reading it a number of times.

It is often said that Dynamite comes in small packages. This is an example that makes the "cliché". An articulate weaving of spiritual and practical knowledge. In fact, you learn, if you didn't know already, that the spiritual truth of God is the most practical of all. If you already knew, you are reinforced and motivated to action in any endeavor in which you are involved. Segarra's writing will increase clarity, confidence and purpose in your life; all in a very quick read that you will enjoy and want to read over and over.

★★★★★ *Must Read!*

This book is very instructive on how we all are accountable for our destiny and how we can improve our relationship with our God by applying the Bible's principles and taking ownership for our acts and thoughts.

★★★★★ *Outstanding reading!!*

This book really was thought-provoking! It brought to the surface many issues I hadn't thought deeply about. I had to read it twice! I am already seeing life in a different way! It's worth your time...read it!

★★★★★ **Essential to your thought life!!!**

This book provides an in depth look at your quality of thought and how it affects the outcome of your life. It is a quick read that contains the keys to unlocking your potential. This is one of those that can change your entire life. Highly Recommended!!!

★★★★★ *Must read!*

An essential book for Christians. An insightful book on spirituality and circumstance.

★★★★★ *Great read!*

I thought this was a fantastic book. The author made strong points and backed it with clear concise thoughts. The reading was easy and thought-provoking. Highly recommend to all those interested in philosophy and religion. Easy to read and very thought-provoking! Candido masterfully weaves philosophy and religion together in captivating manner. Highly recommend!

★★★★★ *A real gem!*

It is often said that Dynamite comes in small packages. This is an example that makes the "cliché". An articulate weaving of spiritual and practical knowledge. In fact, you learn, if you didn't know already, that the spiritual truth of God is the most practical of all. If you already knew, you are reinforced and motivated to action in any endeavor in which you are involved. Segarra's writing will increase clarity, confidence and purpose in your life all in a very quick read that you will enjoy and want to read over and over.

★★★★★ *Unique, enlightening book!!*

This book bought to light issues of deep, penetrating thought. It truly makes you think! Possibilities of personal growth are endless! Worth the read!

★★★★★ *A must read*

Written in such a way that it gives you a spiritual awakening of your thought pattern. I highly recommend this book.

★★★★★ *Very Engaging*

This book helps you see beyond your immediate problems and see the 'bigger picture.' This book will help you to see the timeless principles in the Bible and then apply them to your life.

★★★★★ *Fantastic*

A book with a great blend of spiritual truths and practical thought.

Foresight Book Publishing™

ForesightPublishingNow.com